THE ART OF THE NEW COLD WAR

AMERICA VS. CHINA

WHAT AMERICA MUST DO TO WIN

LEE STEINHAUER

*Dedicated to my son Alexander,
that he may live in a world
led by America and not China.*

CONTENTS

INTRODUCTION

As I write this book, the world is fighting a global pandemic from the COVID-19 virus, which originated in Wuhan, China. The effects of COVID-19 will reverberate long after the health crisis abates, changing the world in countless ways. The pandemic also marks the beginning of the defining event of this century, the clash between America and China, or the New Cold War.

Prior to the onset of the virus, relations between the two nations were already rapidly deteriorating as they engaged in an increasingly heated and prolonged trade war. But the virus, a great accelerator of trends, has further amplified and escalated the underlying tensions between them. The virus may even prove something of a Sputnik moment for Americans, awakening them to the full extent of the China threat, though even without the virus as a catalyst, the clash between America and China was likely inevitable.

The "Thucydides Trap" is a term coined by foreign policy expert Graham Allison to describe the theory that when one great power is rising, it will threaten to displace a more established power. Throughout history, this phenomenon has consistently resulted in war. The examples are myriad: Athens and Sparta, Great Britain and Germany, and many others. China and America are merely the latest example. In ways, however, they are perhaps even more destined to conflict than their predecessors.

China is no ordinary rising great power. For the greater part of human history, China was the world's predominant power. China sees the last two centuries as an historical aberration, and believes it is now returning to its rightful place atop the global food chain. Meanwhile, after vanquishing the Soviet Union in the first Cold War, America became accustomed to unchallenged power, without anything close to a peer rival. This was an historical anomaly itself, causing historians to proclaim the "end of history" as America fashioned its own brand of liberal democracy and free market capitalism onto the world. It underwrote the world's security and prosperity with its unrivaled military might, creating a Pax Americana. Indeed, China's own resurgence owes much to America and the global system it created.

Though China undoubtedly thrived in the American-led world order and the security it provided, it refused to adopt America's governing and economic model, adopting instead an authoritarian style of government and a state-driven economic system. Despite conventional western wisdom, China's authoritarian government produced stability and success to contrast favorably with the frequent messiness and dysfunction of U.S. democracy. China's state-centric economic system not only generated decades of phenomenal growth, but also allowed it to exploit weaknesses inherent in the U.S. economic system. This led other countries, particularly those in the developing world, to ponder whether the China model was superior. And now China offers a new world order to rival the American-led one.

These ingredients make for an epic conflict, in which America, a superpower unlike any other in world history, is pitted against another rising and resurgent superpower with over a billion people that dominated the world for centuries. This is a civilizational clash of East vs. West. And like the first Cold War, the sequel features opposing governing systems and philosophies competing to see which is superior. The New Cold War will be fought intensely on political, economic, and propaganda fronts. It will be fought on global financial markets, in laboratories, and in cyberspace. It will be an all-encompassing strategic competition spanning the entire globe, and may even turn into a hot war in some places.

America prevailed in the first Cold War, but it cannot assume it will prevail in the new one. China is a much different opponent than the Soviet Union, and the world is a much different place. The New Cold War will be far more difficult for America to win than the first. China has studied and learned from the Soviet Union's failure, as well as from America's victory. For the first time ever, America will also be facing an economic peer as a superpower. Indeed, if it continues its current trajectory, China will soon possess the world's largest economy. By certain metrics, China's economy is already the largest.[1]

China is also integrated into the global economy in ways the

Soviet Union never was during the first Cold War. Indeed, China is currently the largest trade partner for many countries in the world, including U.S. allies like Japan and Australia.[2] This poses additional challenges for America in the New Cold War, as well as additional opportunities. And while many of the lessons from the first Cold War are instructive, new strategies must be adopted as well.

This book is entitled *The Art of the New Cold War* as an homage to *The Art of War* by Sun Tzu, which is widely considered the greatest and most influential book on war ever written. Sun Tzu's sage advice and strategies are also highly relevant to the New Cold War, and China is already putting them to use. To prevail, America must learn to do the same.

America must again grow smart and tough and return to the strategic mentality which allowed it to win the first Cold War. To defeat China, America must understand both China's strengths and weaknesses and its own. As Sun Tzu wrote in *The Art of War*:

> "If you know the enemy and know yourself, you need not fear the result of a hundred battles. If you know yourself but not the enemy, for every victory gained you will also suffer a defeat. If you know neither the enemy nor yourself, you will succumb in every battle."

And while China's threat to America is enormous, it also represents an opportunity to make America better and stronger. In a bitterly divided America, the challenge may be the catalyst and unifying force required. Sometimes a worthy competitor is just what the doctor ordered. Indeed, America should be thankful for the challenge presented by China. For as the great Cold War warrior George Kennan once wrote regarding the threat posed to America by the Soviet Union:

"The thoughtful observer of Russian-American relations will find no cause for complaint in the Kremlin's challenge to American society. He will rather experience a certain gratitude to a Providence which, by providing the American people with this implacable challenge, has made their entire security as a nation dependent upon their pulling themselves together and accepting the responsibilities of moral and political leadership that history plainly intended them to bear."

And just as it did in the first Cold War, America must again pull together as a nation and rise to the challenge in the New Cold War. For above all, as General Douglas MacArthur advised, in war, there is no substitute for victory—a maxim exponentially magnified in the New Cold War, because its outcome will change not only America and China, but also the world for centuries to come.

This short book is the product of study, research, and reading over many years. It is informed and influenced by many other books and scholars. To that end, I have provided a reading list at the end of books cited herein, and of others I have found informative. It is also a product of my own thoughts and experiences. I have been fascinated with China and Asia generally since I spent several years living in Singapore as a boy before returning home to America. I have watched China grow and rise through the years with a mixture of awe and trepidation, knowing that one day it would come to threaten my homeland. That day has arrived.

PART I

Know Thy Enemy: The China Threat

CHAPTER 1
A SUPERPOWER REBORN

"The size of China's displacement of the world balance is such that the world must find a new balance. It is not possible to pretend that this is just another big player. This is the biggest player in the history of the world."
– Singapore Prime Minister Lee Kuan Yew, The Grand Master's Insights on China, the United States, and the World by Graham Allison

"We must cultivate China during the next few decades while it is still learning to develop its national strength and potential. Otherwise we will one day be confronted with the most formidable enemy that has ever existed in the history of the world."
– President Richard Nixon

China is a massive continent-sized nation of 1.4 billion people (four times the population of the United States). It is an ancient civilization which has existed in some form for thousands of years. The Middle Kingdom long believed itself to be at the center of the universe, and to be the ruler of everything under Heaven. For much of human history, China lived up to the title.

But over the last two centuries, China has suffered numerous defeats and humiliations. It has been known to the world not as the enlightened center of the universe from which all others can learn, but as a poor backward country. Many blame this precipitous fall on China's closing itself off from the rest of the world, believing it had nothing to learn from foreigners. This proved fatally wrong. Smaller, more technologically advanced foreigners, like the British in the Opium Wars, ravaged China and brought about a Century of Humiliation.

But over the last three decades, China rose again from the ashes to become a superpower. It has transitioned from a poor, largely undeveloped country to the world's second largest economy, and is now on track to become the first. This is an historically unprecedented feat of economic development. How did China do it? Was it simply a restoration of the natural order, or something more than that?

Important lessons emerge when examining China's return to power, one being that America and its largest corporations facilitated China's rise and restoration. U.S. elites also badly misjudged the dragon they had unleashed. Instead of benefiting America by opening a giant new market for its goods and services or creating a new Western-style democracy sharing American beliefs and values, China embraced an illiberal authoritarianism and state-centric economic model, and broke or bent every rule possible to give itself an advantage while exploiting America and its free market system. Indeed, it is no exaggeration to say that China grew strong at America's expense.

Return of the Dragon

China's journey back to superpower status began under Mao Zedong and the Communist Revolution, which gave birth to the People's Republic of China in 1949. Under Mao's leadership, the new China rapidly, if brutally, advanced. It became a nuclear power through the

Great Leap Forward—a ruthless program of forced advancement that killed literally millions of Chinese people. Then, in 1972, the famous meeting between Mao and U.S. President Richard Nixon brought about a normalization of U.S. relations with China, and rapprochement, paving the way for China's economic reengagement with the world.

It was under the reign of Mao's successor Deng Xiaoping in the 1980s and 90s that China began to grow into an economic power and major player in the global economy. Deng instituted the Four Modernizations to spur economic development in China and experimented with market mechanisms while opening the country to foreign investment. China also benefited from optimum conditions for economic development created by the Pax Americana, with the U.S. military keeping peace around the world, and most importantly in China's backyard. This allowed China to concentrate on growing its economy, rather than dealing with external threats.

While China experimented with capitalism and market modernizations under Deng, and saw their fruits, it remained ostensibly a communist nation. This restrained China from fully relinquishing state control of its economy. And while learning the power of capitalism and free markets from the West, China also learned the downsides, including the potential threat it could pose to Chinese Communist Party (CCP) rule. Seeking the best of all worlds, the CCP designed and adopted a hybrid economic model for China—a capitalist system, albeit with the hand of the state controlling its economic development.

Under the Trade Act of 1974, the U.S. officially designated China a non-market economy, a designation including the Soviet Union and other socialist nations. As a result, China could only be granted and enjoy the trade rights and privileges of Most Favored Nation (MFN) status on a conditional basis. China's MFN status was reviewed annually by Congress to ensure that conditions were met. Every year from 1980 through 2000, Congress renewed China's MFN status. However, every year, a debate ensued, with many arguing against renewal for various reasons, including China's human rights violations. This annual uncertainty surrounding renewal restrained U.S. companies from otherwise fully investing in China.[3]

In 2001, though still not yet a market economy, China officially became a member of the World Trade Organization (WTO). China's WTO entry was championed by the U.S. and particularly U.S. companies who had long eyed China's massive emerging market. This permanently relieved the uncertainty surrounding China's MFN status, with WTO members conferring automatic MFN status on each other, among other trading privileges. Entry into the WTO opened the world's markets to China bringing about an export boom and setting the stage for the economic juggernaut we know today.

China's admission into the WTO was a seminal moment for China and the world. It allowed China's economy to grow exponentially by fully accessing and exploiting the fruits of globalization while signaling to the world that China had arrived again as a global power and actor on the world stage. This was also the point at which the relationship between the U.S. and China soured. Indeed, the seeds of the New Cold War can be tracked directly to it.

A Frankenstein

President Nixon feared that he had created a "Frankenstein" by opening the world up to the CCP,[4] a prediction that has in many ways come true. However, if China has become the monster of Nixon's fears, then U.S. elites played the role of its creator, and like the Dr. Frankenstein of Mary Shelley's tale, ultimately lost control of the monster they unleashed.

U.S. elites taught the CCP about all the great benefits of free markets and capitalism. They did not do this out of the goodness of their hearts, but rather to create a China that they could do business with and control. Admitting China to the WTO was the culmination of their goals and was celebrated by U.S. elites as an unmitigated victory. But as it turned out, the victory was the CCP's, while the loss was borne by America's workers.

U.S. elites believed that by entering the WTO, at last, China would become a full market economy. China even made promises to that effect as a prerequisite for entry, committing to lowering trade barriers, not subjecting foreign goods to burdensome regulations or taxes, and protecting intellectual property. Moreover, U.S. elites thought compliance with WTO rules and engagement with free market competition would force China to open its market and liberalize its economy. In short, U.S. elites believed that there was nothing but upside. President Bill Clinton at the time even called it an economic "one-way street," benefitting American workers, consumers, and investors.[5]

But none of this occurred. Instead, China cheated and gamed the WTO system for its own benefit, choosing not to comply with WTO rules that disadvantaged or threatened its state-centric economic model while pursuing aggressive mercantilist trade policies to exploit the WTO's open free trading system, utilizing knowledge of markets taught to them by U.S. elites. And far from being a "one-way street" of benefits for America and its workers, China's entry into the WTO became for many Americans a "one-way street" to job loss and misery.

Prior to entering the WTO, China's exports faced protective tariffs and barriers in the U.S. and other countries. This served to level the playing field and limit China's ability to undercut and flood markets with cheap goods. Upon entering the WTO, however, the tariffs and barriers were lifted, allowing China to fully leverage its near unlimited supply of essentially slave labor to produce and export cheap low margin goods into the world's markets at last.

Like many countries, the U.S. did not sufficiently account for the disruption that adding China to the WTO would bring. Allowing millions of Chinese workers making cheap goods to pour into the world economy had the effect of decimating the U.S. manufacturing sector, putting U.S. workers out of work, with many never able to return to the same income levels and job status again. In his landmark study, MIT economist David Autor attributed the loss of at least a million, if not many more, manufacturing jobs in the U.S. from 1999 to 2011, or about 20 percent of the total job losses in the sector during this period, to the shock of exposure to increased competition from China, which devastated many factory towns in America. [6]

Additionally, as Clyde Prestowitz explains in his excellent book, *The World Turned Upside Down: America, China, and the Struggle for Global Leadership*, by championing China's entry into the WTO, the U.S. government essentially gave the green light to American corporations to fully invest in China, while also guaranteeing that offshoring of production to China and importing formerly American-made goods from China was completely safe and acceptable. Indeed, as Prestowitz puts it bluntly, "they might as well have hung a sign at the White House saying, 'Move to China.'" And many companies did just that.

China's accession to the WTO, and the hundreds of millions of cheap Chinese workers entering the global economy with it, also had significant distortionary effects on the global economy. Some even argue that the 2008-2009 U.S. financial crisis was fueled by these effects. In his book, *China, Trade and Power: Why the West's Economic Engagement with China Has Failed*, economist Stewart

Paterson argues that China's WTO accession, which flooded global markets with cheap labor and goods, led to a supply side shock that triggered deflation. In response, the U.S. Federal Reserve commenced inflation-targeting policies, pumping enormous amounts of extra money into the financial system to combat the deflationary pressures created by China. This in turn resulted in asset price inflation and over-investment in the housing market, which ultimately led to the housing bubble and the attendant financial crisis.

Along with leveraging its inexhaustible supply of cheap labor, China drove down manufacturing costs further relative to the rest of the world with lax environmental and regulatory standards, while strategically devaluing its currency to make its already cheap goods even cheaper in foreign markets. China also provided significant and, in many cases, illegal state subsidies under the WTO to boost exports. As a result, China soon dominated world markets and crushed foreign competitors on its way to becoming the world's largest manufacturer and exporter.

To make matters worse, the U.S. and other WTO countries did not even realize the economic promises of access to China's massive market. For while China gained largely unfettered access to the world's largest markets, it did not provide the same access in return.

Upon entry into the WTO, China insisted on being designated a "developing country." Under WTO rules, developing countries are accorded special and differential treatment, which enabled China to continue to provide subsidies, set higher barriers to market entry, and enact other protections to safeguard its market more than developed economies. China refused to drop this designation even as it grew to the world's second largest economy, a fact that the U.S., most recently under former President Trump, has strongly criticized.[7]

To this day, foreign companies trying to compete in China are severely disadvantaged relative to Chinese domestic companies.

Chinese companies enjoy enormous competitive advantages, including significant subsidies and below-market-rate loans from Chinese state-run banks. Meanwhile, foreign companies face additional regulatory hurdles and barriers that Chinese companies do not. Often, simply as the price of entry to China's market, foreign companies must enter joint ventures with domestic Chinese companies in which they are forced to transfer key technology to their Chinese partner, eventually leading domestic Chinese companies to compete directly against foreign companies using their own technology. And despite their promises, China provides few, if any, protections for foreign companies from intellectual property theft and counterfeiting, resulting in foreign companies being ripped off in China without consequence, costing them billions of dollars each year.

In pursuit of economic strength, China broke or bent every rule, including those it was bound to as a member of the WTO. But no one retaliated against China or brought it to task, not even within the context of the WTO system. Why? Because like a successful mobster, China bought off all the right people, particularly large U.S. companies, which became China's willing accomplices.

The CCP made a very shrewd calculation that for U.S. companies, profits and increasing shareholder value mattered above all else, including their nation's interests. China offered an essentially inexhaustible supply of slave labor to produce products and hardly any environmental or other pesky regulatory standards to drive up costs, and U.S. companies came running, selling out their own country in the process. As manufacturing was outsourced to China, U.S. workers were laid off, decimating America's manufacturing sector. In return, these same companies became China's biggest cheerleaders, lobbying the U.S. government to look the other way on China's numerous abuses.

Wall Street firms also facilitated China's economic abuses. In exchange for sizeable fees, they endorsed and legitimized Chinese companies with questionable, or even fraudulent, accounting practices and unreliable financial statements, assisting them in circumventing regulatory requirements and legal disclosures to allow them to tap into capital markets and list on public stock exchanges. Wall Street firms also deliberately covered up the fact that many were directly owned and controlled by the CCP.

U.S. politicians of both political parties aided and abetted China's economic rule breaking as well, not only due to intense lobbying by U.S. companies and their significant campaign donations, but also because Washington elites badly misjudged China. They believed entry into the WTO would result in political and market reforms in China, and that China would become an important ally and stakeholder in the U.S.-led system. This would ultimately cause China to even become more democratic—in a word, more like America.

Instead of westernizing, however, as U.S. elites had believed, the CCP took China in the opposite direction, becoming ever more authoritarian. And far from reforming and liberalizing their economy, private enterprise and free market mechanisms in China were increasingly crowded out in favor of massive state-owned and state-controlled enterprises, making true the Chinese saying, "the state advances as the private sector retreats."

The CCP became particularly emboldened after the 2008-2009 financial crisis that crushed the western world. They came to believe—even openly pronounced—that their authoritarian form of governance and state-controlled capitalist system were superior to the U.S. governance and economic model. A top Chinese official at the time even remarked to then U.S. Treasury Secretary Hank Paulson, "you were our teacher—and our teacher doesn't look very smart!"[8]

Now, at every turn, China is openly and aggressively challenging U.S. leadership around the globe, even the U.S.-led system itself. In every strategic sphere, China is leveraging its growing economic might to overtake America, posing the greatest threat to America and the free world since the Soviet Union.

CHAPTER 2

XI'S QUEST FOR GLOBAL DOMINATION

"Therefore the skillful leader subdues the enemy's troops without any fighting; he captures their cities without laying siege to them; he overthrows their kingdom without lengthy operations in the field." – Sun Tzu, *The Art of War*

"Where Western strategists reflect on the means to assemble superior power at the decisive point, Sun Tzu addresses the means of building a dominant political and psychological position, such that the outcome of a conflict becomes a foregone conclusion. Western strategists test their maxims by victories in battles; Sun Tzu tests by victories where battles have become unnecessary." – Henry Kissinger, *On China*

As discussed at the beginning of this book, the "Thucydides Trap" is the term coined by foreign policy expert Graham Allison to describe the concept that when one great power is rising, it will inevitably threaten to displace the established power. Throughout history, this has consistently resulted in war. The examples are myriad: Athens and Sparta, Great Britain and Germany, and many others. Under this theory, China and America are perhaps fated to conflict.

Foreign policy expert Christopher Layne, writing in the November 2020 edition of *Foreign Affairs* magazine, in a piece entitled "The Return of Great-Power War," highlights stark parallels between pre-1914 British-German relations, ultimately resulting in World War I, and contemporary U.S.-China relations. Layne explains how in the early twentieth century, as Germany grew into an economic and technological power, Great Britain, the world's foremost power at the time, felt increasingly threatened. According to Layne, however, Germany desired only an appropriate seat at the table commensurate with its growing power, and did not seek to be Great Britain's enemy, merely to be viewed as an equal in the world. In the end, though, despite vast economic and cultural connections between the two powers, Great Britain simply could not countenance losing its dominant position to a historically lesser power.

Layne of course sees modern day America in the position of pre-1914 Great Britain—as an established hegemon accustomed to unrivaled power suddenly threatened by an upstart challenger in China. This raises the question of whether history will repeat itself, as a declining America attempts to stop a rising China from becoming its equal or superior.

In drawing parallels between China and pre-1914 Germany, Layne implies that China, like Germany only desires an equal seat at the table commensurate with its size and power. Layne and others may therefore view China's actions as merely appropriate for a growing superpower bestriding the world, and perhaps even argue, as others have before, that when America was rising to power under President Teddy Roosevelt, it engaged in similar behavior. Thus, it will ultimately be America's choice whether to fall into the Thucydides Trap by going to war to arrest what China has charitably termed its "peaceful rise."

This view, however, does not provide for a complete or accurate picture of the state of relations between the two superpower nations. Indeed, historically speaking, America, not China, is the upstart challenger to the throne, which belonged to China for centuries. To China, the natural order is simply being restored—a historical aberration being corrected after a Century of Humiliation at the hands of western nations. To achieve this long-awaited restoration, China is hardly a benign actor, as suggested, but one actively engaged in seeing it come to fruition. This process includes weakening the greatest obstacle standing in its way—America. Nor does China desire only an equal seat at America's table. Rather, as we shall see quite clearly, China seeks instead to overturn the table completely, by any means necessary.

China's Clandestine War

While the West plays Chess, the Chinese play an ancient game called Go, a game of strategy in which the goal is to surround and occupy more territory than your opponent through the course of the contest. In many ways, China has been playing a game of Go with America and the world, unbeknownst to both.

China is even keeping score through a metric called Comprehensive National Power (CNP). CNP is the sum of a nation's overall strength, as measured by a wide range of factors, including economic power, military power, human capital, natural resources, science and technology, and influence (soft power). The combination composes a nation's CNP. The higher the CNP, the stronger the nation.

The Chinese Communist Party (CCP) systematically computes and measures CNP, implementing policies based upon it, and gauging the success of those policies by whether CNP is increased or decreased. The CCP does everything possible to increase China's CNP, while also seeking to decrease other nations' CNP relative to China's. This is particularly true when it comes to America. The

CCP has waged what some scholars claim to be a clandestine strategic war to degrade U.S. capabilities so China can overtake the U.S. as the world's strongest nation.

The most famous and influential of these scholars is Michael Pillsbury. In his seminal work *The Hundred-Year Marathon: China's Secret Strategy to Replace America as the Global Superpower*, Pillsbury argues that China has engaged in a strategic war against America for decades. According to Pillsbury, the hundred-year marathon is China's grand strategy, which began under Mao. Its aim is to supplant America as the world's dominant power by 2049, the one-hundredth anniversary of the founding of the People's Republic. Retired U.S. Air Force Brigadier General Robert Spalding makes this claim as well in his book, *Stealth War: How China Took Over While America's Elite Slept*.

Some even assert that the first Cold War never really ended, or rather that only the European phase did, while the Asian phase is still ongoing. The aims of the CCP are the same as the Soviet Union's were: to replace America as the world's leading economic and military power and ultimately achieve a monopoly on world power. Indeed, communists, like the CCP, understand and conceptualize war differently from America, as a far broader conflict, encompassing political, psychological, cultural, economic, and subversive aspects.[9]

To that end, many, including Pillsbury and Spalding, believe the CCP is following the playbook set forth in *Unrestricted Warfare*, a book on military strategy written by two Chinese colonels in the 1990s. The book, which extends many of Sun Tzu's precepts to the modern age, advises on how China can defeat America, a militarily and technologically superior opponent. As the name suggests, the book promotes warfare transcending traditional battlefields and concepts of warfare, envisioning war as limitless and everywhere, encompassing all means and facets of society, and blurring lines between soldiers and civilians.

Recognizing that China would lose a direct military conflict with America, at the time by far and away the world's greatest military power, the book's authors advocated that China covertly utilize political, psychological, cultural, economic, and subversive aspects to compromise and degrade America's position over time, thereby circumventing the need for direct military action, and ultimately causing America to grow strategically weak, while conversely allowing China time to grow strategically strong, so China's victory became a *fait accompli*. This allowed China to win the war without a single shot ever being fired, and fulfilled two of Sun Tzu's most important maxims: "to subdue the enemy without fighting is the acme of skill" and "every battle is won or lost before it is ever fought."

For over two decades, the CCP has successfully carried out the strategy set forth in *Unrestricted Warfare*, while U.S. elites and policymakers have remained oblivious, or, in some cases, willfully ignorant. It was not until recently that U.S. officials became aware of China's plot through the scholarship of Pillsbury, Spalding, and others, and finally publicly acknowledged the CCP's hegemonic designs and decades-long clandestine strategic war to supplant America as the world's dominant power.

Acknowledgement came in the summer of 2020, in the form of a series of four Cold War-esque speeches given by top Trump administration officials. The purpose of these speeches "was to explain the different facets of America's relationship with China, the massive imbalances in that relationship that have built up over decades, and the Chinese Communist Party's designs for hegemony."[10] FBI Director Christopher Wray's speech focused on the CCP's belief that they are in a "generational fight" to make China "the world's only superpower by any means necessary."[11] National Security Advisor

Robert O'Brien outlined how the CCP seeks to export its ideology and "control thought beyond its borders."[12] Attorney General William Barr focused on economic aspects, specifically the CCP's longtime theft of America's intellectual property and trade secrets. As Barr put it bluntly, "The ultimate ambition of China's rulers isn't to trade with the United States. It is to raid the United States."[13] Finally, Secretary of State Mike Pompeo, bringing all three speeches together, declared publicly for the first time that Xi Jinping and the CCP are engaged in a decades-long battle against the U.S. for global supremacy.[14]

The New Red Emperor

For many years, the CCP kept its intentions and plans for global hegemony hidden from America and the world as China gathered its strength. Following Deng Xiaoping's prescient advice to "hide our capacities and bide our time," the CCP was content to quietly grow strong while its great rival grew weak, even feigning its own weakness so as not to draw unwanted attention, while adhering to Sun Tzu's maxim "to appear weak when you are strong." But all that changed in 2012 when Xi Jinping ascended to China's presidency.

Xi is the strongest and most powerful CCP leader since Mao, and in many ways Xi is following in the Great Helmsman's footsteps. Upon ascending to the presidency, Xi implemented a massive Maoist-like purge in the name of combating corruption to ruthlessly eliminate potential rivals to his power. Xi has now effectively made himself president for life, and is often referred to as the "Chairman of Everything" in China, having centralized and concentrated all levels of power into his person. Indeed, his very "thoughts" are now enshrined in China's constitution, and must be studied and followed.

Like Mao, Xi is an ideologue and CCP hardliner, and is reasserting CCP control over all aspects of Chinese life. According to Xi's governing philosophy, called "Xi Jinping Thought on Socialism with Chinese Characteristics for a New Era," which is now enshrined in the party's constitution: "Government, the military, society and schools, north, south, east and west—the party leads them all."[15] Indeed, CCP control is now fully evident in all aspects of China's society, including the economy, where the state has taken an ever expansive and active role, with the market reforms implemented under Deng Xiaoping largely undone.

Xi demands that private enterprise, and indeed the entire Chinese economy, serve the CCP's strategic interests and goals. Under him, China has gone from what some once called China Inc. to what some now call CCP Inc.[16] By effectively erasing any distinctions or clear demarcations between state-owned and private companies, the CCP has systematically expanded its role in every part of the economy. Even ostensibly private companies in China are increasingly influenced or outright controlled by the CCP, to the point where it is almost impossible to delineate where CCP influence ends and firm autonomy begins.[17]

Viewing economic power as national power, Xi is an aggressive practitioner of economic statecraft, wielding China's market and companies as weapons in the pursuit of political and geopolitical ends. To Xi, commerce and trade are but extensions of politics and the state. Under him, China's massive state-owned enterprises (SOEs), some of the biggest and most powerful companies in the world, act effectively as arms of the state. Directed by the CCP, Chinese SOEs make investments going beyond mere commercial considerations to encompass the CCP's larger strategic and geopolitical goals. For example, Chinese SOEs have invested in and acquired ports and other critical infrastructure throughout the world, allowing China and the CCP to now control global infrastructure to a degree that previous empires only accomplished through military conquest. Chinese SOEs also make strategic investments in companies throughout the world for the sole purpose of obtaining cutting edge technology, intellectual property, and natural resources for China.

Moreover, under Xi, any economic tie whatsoever with China is leveraged and weaponized by the CCP as a tool of political coercion and influence, which many foreign companies, including major U.S. corporations, have quickly discovered. The CCP frequently engages in the economic equivalent of hostage taking, threatening foreign companies with shutting down their plants and operations in China and denying them access to the Chinese market if they do not transfer their technology, enter joint ventures with Chinese companies, build and invest in China, or rectify any transgression whatsoever. Indeed, it is often said that U.S. companies fear challenging Beijing far more than they do Washington.

Under Xi, countries fall victim to the CCP's economic coercion as well. For example, when South Korea agreed to install a U.S. missile defense system, South Korean products and companies were boycotted in China.[18] And in 2019, in response to a tweet from Houston Rockets General Manager Daryl Morey supporting freedom fighters in Hong Kong, Chinese companies cancelled licensing deals for the team's merchandise, and the CCP banned all broadcasts of NBA games.[19] Most recently, onerous tariffs were placed on key Australian goods after they had the audacity to request an investigation into the Chinese origins of the coronavirus.[20]

Emboldened by China's growing economic and geopolitical power, Xi has completely discarded Deng Xiaoping's long held advice to "hide our capacities and bide our time." Xi believes China's time has arrived and has proclaimed a new guiding motto for China: Xi's "China Dream," a perversion of the "American Dream." Xi's dream, like Mao's before him, is China's returning to its rightful place and once again taking "center stage in the world."

To achieve his China Dream, Xi has taken direct aim at U.S. leadership, and like a geopolitical game of Go, is surrounding the world economically, politically, technologically, and militarily. Specifically, Xi is doing this through three overlapping and complementary strategic policies: Made in China 2025 (MIC25), Military-Civil Fusion Strategy (MCF), and the Belt Road and Initiative (BRI).

MIC25, MCF, & BRI

China grew into the second largest economy by becoming the world's workshop, and exporting low margin, low tech goods. But Xi understands that true power comes from innovation and cutting-edge technology, not from making and selling shoes and t-shirts. Xi knows that so long as the U.S. dominates high-tech industries, it will lead the world. To remedy this, in 2015, Xi announced a new strategic industrial policy called the Made in China 2025 plan. MIC25 is China's blueprint for becoming a technological superpower and achieving tech supremacy over the U.S. The plan seeks to develop "national champion" companies as global leaders in ten priority industries by 2025. These industries include: (1) AI, quantum computing, and next-generation information technology; (2) robotics and automation; (3) aerospace and space; (4) high-tech shipping and oceanic engineering; (5) high-speed railway; (6) energy efficiency; (7) new materials; (8) biotechnology, medical devices, and advanced pharmaceuticals; (9) next-generation energy and power generation; and (10) agricultural machinery.[21]

To achieve MIC25, Xi is injecting billions of dollars in state financing and subsidies into companies in priority industries, while also seeking to obtain cutting edge technology and intellectual property from across the world. For this purpose, he has ordered state-owned enterprises to make strategic investments in emerging tech companies while continuing to force technology transfers from foreign companies operating in China. What cannot be obtained through lawful means or coercion is stolen through state-sponsored cybertheft and espionage, with America and its companies often the prime target.

According to the FBI, the Chinese government is implicated in around 60 percent of all trade secret theft cases in America.[22] FBI Director Christopher Wray even projected that his agency is "opening a new China-related counterintelligence case about every 10 hours."[23] China's rampant theft of technology and intellectual property has cost America and its companies enormously. General Keith Alexander, the former director of the National Security Agency, described China's cybertheft of American technology as the "greatest transfer of wealth in history."[24] And a June 2018 White House Office of Trade and Manufacturing Policy Report estimated the annual cost to the U.S. economy of China's theft of intellectual property and trade secrets to be as high as $600 billion.[25]

China also obtains foreign technology through its Thousand Talents Program (TTP), an extensive recruitment program that incentivizes individuals engaged in research and development in America and other countries to transmit knowledge and research to China. A 2019 staff report to the United States Senate Subcommittee on Homeland Security and Governmental Affairs extensively details how "American taxpayer-funded research has contributed to China's global rise over the last 20 years," as China recruited "U.S. based researchers, scientists, and experts in the public and private sector to provide China with knowledge and intellectual capital in exchange for monetary gain and other benefits."[26] According to the report, TTP has attracted more than 7,000 individuals and is only one of almost 200 similar Chinese talent recruitment programs operating throughout the world.

Xi is using coerced and stolen technology to transform China's economy as well as its military. Through a strategy of military-civil fusion (MCF), Xi aims to develop the world's most advanced military by 2049. MCF is a military industrial complex on steroids, leveraging all aspects of state and commercial power to strengthen and advance the military. MCF blurs if not outright erases lines between China's military and civilian sectors, and as the name suggests, fuses the civilian and military domains, eliminating any distinctions between military and economic resources.

To further MCF, Xi passed a National Intelligence Law compelling companies and individuals in China to assist with state security and national intelligence and requiring new technologies developed by the private sector be shared with the military. Of particular interest are dual-use technologies with both economic and military application.

One important dual use technology is artificial intelligence (A.I.). Xi believes A.I. will drive the next generation of warfare and enable China to leapfrog over America in both economic and military supremacy, an assessment supported by A.I. experts, who, like Xi, believe that whichever country leads in A.I. will surpass all others. In 2017, Xi instituted a national development plan for China to become the world leader in A.I. by 2030.[27] The plan includes a multibillion-dollar national investment to support moonshot projects, start-ups, and academic research in A.I.[28]

A.I. expert Dr. Kai Fu Lee argues in his book *AI Superpowers: China, Silicon Valley, and the New World Order* that China is poised to become the global leader in A.I. not only because of its aggressive investment and acquisition of A.I. technology but also because of its vast data collection. Data is the fuel that drives A.I., and no other country is as voracious in acquiring data as China. With 1.4 billion people, very few privacy laws restricting companies or the government from acquiring data from individuals, a vast surveillance state, and a largely digitized society, China produces and collects more data than anyone in the world. Simply put, if data is the oil that powers A.I., then China is Saudi Arabia.

Another critical dual use technology China is racing ahead in is 5G. Short for fifth-generation wireless, experts believe 5G could spearhead the next industrial revolution. Vastly faster than today's 4G networks, 5G could be the key to innovations and future technologies such as driverless cars, robot-run factories, and all sorts of advanced weaponry.[29] Xi is using China's largest telecommunication company and national champion Huawei to dominant 5G markets across the world. An archetype of MIC25 and MCF, Huawei is enhanced by stolen technology and billions in state subsidies. Xi is intent on exploiting Huawei's growing market share in 5G technology to build digital infrastructure and network services in countries throughout the world, enabling Huawei, and by extension the CCP, to siphon and exploit data transmitted over these systems, effectively granting the CCP enormous control over these countries and their security.

The push to build and control digital infrastructure is a central component of Xi's Belt and Road Initiative (BRI). Announced in 2013, BRI is China's New Silk Road, named after the original Silk Road of ancient times which forged trading networks throughout Central Asia and into India and Europe. An enormously ambitious project, currently spanning 140 countries and counting, BRI envisions a vast network of transportation, energy, and telecommunications infrastructure linking Europe, Africa, and Asia. Through trillions in new infrastructure investments in developing countries, BRI is intended to place China at the center of critical trade routes and communications networks. And as Henry Kissinger puts it, it will "shift the world's center of gravity from the Atlantic to the Pacific."[30]

BRI has both economic and foreign policy strategic dimensions for China. Not only is BRI opening new markets for Chinese goods, but also, it is binding countries to China through debt trap diplomacy and predatory lending practices. Developing countries have discovered to their detriment that China's investment comes with significant strings attached. China demands massive collateral for its loans, and when debtor nations cannot pay their debts, China seizes their natural resources and critical infrastructure. For instance, in 2017, Sri Lanka was forced to hand over a port to China to pay off its BRI debts.[31] By making countries debtors, China controls and molds them to its will, including forcing debtor nations to align with the CCP's geopolitical agenda and preferred value system, for example on human and privacy rights.

Through BRI, Xi is also forging a China-led sphere of influence by creating world shaping international norms and institutions. In 2016, China launched the Asian Infrastructure Investment Bank (AIIB) to support BRI. Despite American and Japanese opposition, 87 other countries signed up as charter members to offer financing to BRI infrastructure projects. Billed as the China-led version of the World Bank, AIIB takes direct aim at the Bretton Woods system, established under the leadership of America after World War II, by launching an alternative and rival system led by China. In conjunction, BRI is also being used to expand international use of China's currency, the renminbi, with the ultimate objective of unseating the U.S. dollar as the world's reserve currency.

Last but not least, Xi is using BRI to export the CCP's governance and development model, creating an alternative vision for global leadership designed to challenge U.S. dominance. Xi has exploited crises like the western financial crisis and the COVID-19 pandemic to push the superiority of the China model. China also provides significant financial and other incentives to developing countries·for adoption of their model, even offering training to the leaders of developing countries while selling them the cyber and surveillance tools to repress their citizens.[32] As a result, the China model is rapidly gaining traction throughout the developing world, and increasingly becoming the dominant model for governance and development.

★ ★ ★

From every conceivable angle, an emboldened China is now openly and aggressively challenging America across the board—economically, politically, militarily, and technologically—in ways rivaling even the Soviet Union at the height of the first Cold War. To further emphasize the point, the CCP's latest five-year plan even sets forth a special 15-year strategy called "Vision 2035," with the explicit goal of equaling or overtaking the U.S. in nearly every facet of power within the next fifteen years.[33] It is therefore without question that China not only seeks to be America's rival, but also that it aims to be, in due course, its superior. And like the ancient Chinese proverb says, "there cannot be two suns in one sky."

Now that we have set forth the enormous challenge presented by China, we begin to turn our attention to America. Specifically, we must focus on what America must do to fight back against China and win the New Cold War.

The mere posing of the question implies that America will not win if it does not make changes. Otherwise, the rest of this book would be superfluous. America does indeed need to make changes to successfully confront China. The first of these is to fully realize the extent of the China threat. America must understand the stark reality that it can lose to China, and that victory is far from assured. Indeed, if America does not make the necessary changes and take the necessary actions, it *will* lose.

The good news is that the COVID-19 pandemic has alerted Americans to the China threat. There are still some, of course, who remain delusional about China and its intentions. Perhaps there will always be a certain number who are. But those in power must not be among them.

Realization of the China threat, though necessary, is far from sufficient. Bold actions must also be taken, and America must adapt to a changing world. In many ways, America must even take a page or two from China's playbook, just as China learned from America to grow strong. America must become far more strategic. It must concentrate on and enhance core strengths. It must exit strategically stupid and inconsequential conflicts throughout the world. It must marshal and utilize resources much more effectively. It must adapt and modify its economy, military, foreign policy, education, and immigration systems to the war against China. In short, America must take a whole government, "kitchen sink" approach to China, weaponizing and mobilizing every aspect of American society against China, just as China has against America.

The following chapters will discuss each of the major areas that America will need to address to win. Admittedly, each subject could constitute a book in and of itself. But for the scope of this book, and for the sake of brevity, each area is discussed broadly.

First, however, we must examine the two competing systems of government, comparing the strengths and weaknesses of each, for those strengths and weaknesses may determine which nation prevails in the New Cold War. And for America especially, its system of government, and whether it can overcome the serious challenges it faces, will determine the extent to which it can enact the changes and measures necessary to defeat China.

CHAPTER 3

U.S. DEMOCRACY VS. CHINESE AUTOCRACY: TALE OF THE TAPE

*"The most terrifying words in the English language are:
I'm from the government and I'm here to help."*
– President Ronald Reagan

*"You know, the cure for all this talk is really a good dose of
incompetent government. You get that alternative and you'll
never put Singapore together again: Humpty Dumpty
cannot be put together again... my asset values will disappear,
my apartments will be worth a fraction of what they were,
my ministers' jobs will be in peril, their security will be
at risk and their women will become maids in other
people's countries, foreign workers. I cannot have that!"*
– Lee Kuan Yew on justifying a million-dollar pay increase
for Singapore ministers

The quotes above, the first from U.S. President Ronald Reagan, and the second from Singapore Prime Minister Lee Kuan Yew, convey two diametrically opposed perspectives on and philosophies of government.

Lee Kuan Yew's quote came in relation to justifying a mil-lion-dollar pay increase for his top government officials, a proposition virtually unheard of in America, which if ever proposed would be derided as a gross wasting of taxpayer dollars. But Lee Kuan Yew saw it as exactly the opposite. If unable to retain top talent in government, he believed the entire country would suffer egregiously, as the government would soon be run by incompetents. He also believed that by paying his officials well, not only would he attract and retain top talent, but also, he would deter them from being tempted by corruption or leveraging their positions in the private sector. Regardless of whether one subscribes to Lee Kuan Yew's assessment, what is undoubtedly true is that under his leadership Singapore became—in very short order—an extremely successful, influential, and wealthy country, a remarkable achievement for a small island nation with few natural resources established less than a century ago.

President Ronald Reagan, on the other hand, famously believed that government caused far more problems than solutions. According to Reagan, government itself was the problem. The less government, therefore, the better. And Reagan ushered in a conservative movement in America intent upon shrinking it.

Thus, we have two highly successful leaders setting forth two very different viewpoints of government. Undoubtedly, there is a cultural element at play, and the style of government over which each presided was quite different, as was its historical basis. Where they both agree, however, is that bad government, resulting from either too much government or the incompetence of those in government, presents a dire threat to a nation and its people.

This is especially true with regards to war. A weak or incompetent government during peacetime can hinder a nation, but one presiding during wartime can end a nation. Government is therefore an all-important consideration in the New Cold War, as the vitality of the two competing systems of government will define in large part whether China or America ultimately triumphs.

The New Cold War, like the first, will again feature a battle between a democracy and an autocracy. In the first Cold War, U.S. democracy was superior to the Soviet Union's autocratic communist party system; a fact in the end decisive as the Soviet political system literally collapsed, along with the entire Union. Will history repeat itself in the New Cold War? Or does China's brand of autocracy have the advantage?

To answer this question, we measure the "tale of the tape," comparing the Chinese Communist Party with U.S. democracy, highlighting the advantages and disadvantages of each, along with the threats and challenges each one faces.

The Chinese Communist Party (CCP)

China is an authoritarian one-party state, ruled absolutely by the Chinese Communist Party (CCP). When westerners think of the communist party, it conjures images of the Soviet Union and its great historic failures. Viewed through this lens, hardly any would consider communist party rule to be a strength. But while there are unquestionably weaknesses inherent in the CCP system, just as there were in the Soviet Union's, it is also undeniable that the CCP has proven by many measures a great success, even a strategic asset for China in the New Cold War.

Firstly, it must be acknowledged that the CCP is not the communist party of the Soviet Union. The CCP is far more competent, better organized, and adaptive. The CCP has also studied deeply and learned the lessons of the Soviet Union's failure, so as not to repeat them. They have also learned the positive governance lessons from the successful rise of the so-called Asian Tigers, including Singapore, and incorporated them. And in a massive continent sized nation of 1.4 billion people, the CCP can justifiably tout tremendous economic and developmental success under its leadership, lifting millions from poverty and restoring the nation to glory.

The CCP functions much like a corporation, and for that reason President Xi Jinping is often referred to as the CEO of China, including by China scholar Kerry Brown in his book *CEO, China: The Rise of Xi Jinping.* Xi also chairs China's ostensible Board of Directors, the 25-member Politburo which serves as the nation's primary decision-making body. Like a successful corporation, entry into the CCP is extremely competitive, as it recruits the best and brightest from elite schools to enter its ranks. According to Kerry Brown, even President Xi successfully applied to enter the CCP only after ten failed attempts.

The CCP rigorously trains its future leaders, putting them through elite party run schools and assigning them increasingly difficult positions to prove themselves, ensuring their competency. In the CCP system, a Donald Trump, never having held elected office, or a Barack Obama, only serving one term as a Senator, would have never been allowed to hold any significant leadership positions, let alone that of President. A potential CCP leader begins by governing a small village. Then, if they prove themselves in that position, they may be promoted to govern a slightly larger municipality, where once again they must prove themselves, and so on and so forth, graduating to progressively larger responsibility as they climb the leadership ladder. This process results, by and large, in highly competent leadership in China. This is extremely important, as by design, the CCP is integral to China's success or failure and enmeshed to a significant degree in all aspects of Chinese society.

The CCP possesses limitless power in China, and has no political opposition whatsoever. Indeed, the entire government apparatus, even China's military, is not only completely controlled by the CCP but also set up for the sole purpose of keeping the CCP in power. Unconcerned with reelection, whims of voters, attacks by opposition political parties or special interests, the CCP can implement long term strategic plans and goals and marshal unbelievable resources towards achieving them. And where one might expect such a system to become overly bureaucratic, rigid, stale, and subject to group think, like that of the Soviet Union, the CCP has proven remarkably adaptable and even in some ways responsive to its citizens.

The CCP is also of course a brutal authoritarian regime which harshly suppresses the rights of its citizens, crushes any semblance of opposition, and has turned China into a virtual Orwellian surveillance state where just posting an unfavorable meme about President Xi on social media results in severe punishment. Human rights violations are also an everyday occurrence, with minority groups like the Uighurs forced into mass internment camps by the hundreds of thousands. These actions cause other countries to distrust the CCP and recoil from engaging in closer relations with China, weakening its hand internationally.

Despite the oppression, the CCP enjoys the overwhelming support of the Chinese people and continues to possess the Mandate of Heaven—an important ancient Chinese concept signifying that the ruler has the blessing of the gods. The reason is that the CCP has entered into an implicit social contract with the Chinese people—so long as economic development continues, and standards of living rise, the CCP enjoys free rein in politics. So far, this contract remains intact, and is a price the Chinese people are willing to pay for growing prosperity and stature in the world. There are, however, serious challenges ahead which may upset this arrangement.

The Chinese economy has grown phenomenally year after year for decades, enjoying perhaps more than any other nation the fruits of globalization. But economic growth is starting to slow and appears poised to continue to do so. The CCP has attempted to continually juice economic growth through debt-driven public investment in infrastructure, though even that is now losing its potency, and is otherwise unsustainable with many investments non-performing, leading to infamous so-called ghost cities throughout China with blocks of completely empty buildings. As a result, the CCP has sought to not only open new markets through its Belt and Road Initiative but also to stimulate greater domestic consumption in China, most recently through a "dual circulation" strategy focused on boosting and developing the Chinese domestic market. This has not been an easy task, however, as the Chinese people, though growing richer, remain poor on a per capita basis, with millions living on less than a few dollars a day. Additionally, there is little to no modern social safety net in China, resulting in Chinese people saving disproportionately instead of spending. This problem is exacerbated by China's rapidly aging population and decades long one-child policy that have left it without an adequate number of younger workers to replace and support retiring ones. China is thus growing old before it grows rich. Ultimately, this will require the CCP to spend enormous sums on creating a massive social safety net, which may considerably constrain its ability to prop up the economy through public investment or other growth-enhancing measures.

Enormous income inequalities in China have also grown between urban elites living in thriving metropolises and impoverished Chinese peasants living in rural areas, a problem made worse by endemic corruption by CCP members who have enriched themselves at the expense of the people. Chinese peasants have long suffered from land expropriation by CCP officials and well-connected land developers, and land is cited by the Chinese government as the greatest source of "mass social conflict" in China today.[34] To remedy this situation, massive land reforms will be needed—including the granting of property rights to peasants—which will be politically and logistically difficult. If not remedied, though, land and the inequalities it has bred will continue to provide the spark for social tensions.

The foregoing factors, among others, may imperil the CCP's system of governance in the future and the bargain underpinning it. And while currently the CCP appears all-powerful, that may not be the case going forward, especially as the economic development glossing over other serious societal problems slows. The New Cold War may also serve to expose and accelerate these factors. Indeed, it is in America's strategic interest to do so.

The CCP may also ultimately end up a victim of its own success, for historically, as countries grow richer, citizens demand a greater say in governance. How will the CCP adjust when this occurs? For a regime built upon the premise of total control, it is unlikely to be an easy transition. For guidance, one need only look to the 1989 Tiananmen Square tragedy, or recently, the turmoil in Hong Kong, to see how the CCP reacts to political challenges.

The CCP has already started preparing for these challenges by enacting greater forms of control over the Chinese people. In fact, the CCP spends hundreds of billions of dollars every year just for this purpose. It censors the internet through the Great Chinese Firewall, implementing surveillance systems to monitor citizens, and recently established a "social credit" system to reward and punish behavior. It is likely even more aggressive measures will be taken in future if the CCP feels its grip slipping or social tensions rising, increasingly diverting resources and focus to the preservation of domestic order, and potentially hindering the CCP's ability to wage war against America and assert power globally.

In sum, for now, at least, the CCP appears well positioned from a governance standpoint in the New Cold War. The same of course could have been said about the Soviet Union at various stages of the first Cold War. The test will be whether it can be sustained throughout the course of the New Cold War, which there is certainly considerable reason to doubt. But whether potential deficiencies in the Chinese system can be capitalized upon by America greatly depends on the efficacy of America's own system of government, and whether it can overcome its own considerable threats and challenges.

U.S. Democracy

Winston Churchill famously said, "Democracy is the worst form of government, except for all the others." In the arc of history, Churchill's quip has rung true. Democracy, by most metrics, has proven the best form of government, in relation, at least, to the others. Democracies, or more precisely, constitutional republics electing their representatives democratically, are the strongest, most successful, most prosperous nations over the last century, exemplified of course by America.

However, democracy has not been without its weaknesses. Even when functioning at its very best, it can be messy and illogical, and in relation to autocracies like China, agonizingly slow and inefficient. U.S. democracy suffers these weaknesses acutely. As a result, many experts view the U.S. political system as a potential liability in the New Cold War, including former U.S. Treasury Secretary and China hand Hank Paulson, who even remarked that the U.S. political system represents the greatest threat to U.S. predominance.[35]

Others, however, take the opposite view, one being Mathew Kroenig in his excellent book *The Return of Great Power Rivalry: Democracy versus Autocracy from the Ancient World to the U.S. and China,* in which he hypothesizes that in great power rivalries throughout history, democracies consistently defeat autocracies.

Kroenig references numerous examples to support this proposition, including America's defeat of Japan and Nazi Germany in WWII and the Soviet Union in the first Cold War, and going back to antiquity to wars fought by Athens and Rome. Kroenig argues that democracies enjoy certain advantages over autocracies, including the ability to attract other democracies as trusted and lasting allies; openness leading to economic dynamism and innovation; good decision-making stemming from accountability; and the ability to adapt and self-correct. Kroenig's arguments would be echoed approvingly by America's Founding Fathers, who designed the U.S. political system with the advantages he cites in mind. And what others might see as the U.S. political system's inherent weaknesses, the Founders, like Kroenig, saw as its greatest strengths.

America's Founders could not possibly have anticipated all the changes, technological and otherwise, that the world has experienced since drafting the U.S. Constitution in the late 1700s, nor did they ever think they could. As students of history and philosophy, however, what they understood keenly were the fundamental truths of power and human nature, which have remained unchanged since ancient times. They applied and incorporated these fundamental truths into the political system they designed.

The Founders' philosophy on government is perhaps best summed up by Founding Father James Madison in the *Federalist Papers*:

"If men were angels, no government would be necessary. If angels were to govern men, neither external nor internal controls on government would be necessary. In framing a government which is to be administered by men over men, the great difficulty lies in this: you must first enable the government to control the governed; and the next place, oblige it to control itself."

The Founders understood that just as government was required to restrain the worst impulses of the people it governed, government in turn must be restrained from itself and its own worst impulses. The Founders experienced firsthand the dangers of unrestrained government at the hands of the British, against whom they fought a war to break free. To safeguard against the dangers of an all-powerful, overly expansive government, they devised for America a limited government with separation of powers and checks and balances to preserve the liberty and freedom they so cherished. These restraints were not intended to impede America's ability to possess a strong and well-functioning government or a well-functioning society. To the contrary, they were to ensure both.

Many of the Founders were businessman, inventors, and entrepreneurs painfully aware of an overbearing government's penchant to stifle private enterprise and innovation through burdensome overregulation and high taxation. Meanwhile, individual citizens free of government control and possessing freedom, liberty, and opportunity could create, build, and be rewarded for their risk taking. These free citizens would invent the industries and technologies of the future, enriching the entire nation. So it was that the Founders wanted an entrepreneurial culture and spirit to thrive in America, to become what we might term in our modern nomenclature a start-up nation. Therefore, in creating a limited form of government, the Founders embraced, even built into the system, dynamism, innovation, and a pioneering spirit, a goal achieved as America became in short order the world's most innovative nation.

Winston Churchill also once famously quipped, "Americans will always do the right thing, only after they have tried everything else." This was perhaps a backhanded compliment, but also one indicative of the U.S. political system's remarkable ability to correct its own course. The Founders designed the system to be resilient and adaptable, even "antifragile," a term coined by modern day philosopher Nassim Nicholas Taleb to define resilient systems that gain and grow stronger from disorder and stressors. And indeed, throughout its history, the U.S. political system has proven extraordinarily resilient in the face of adversity, a key reason why America possesses the world's oldest continuous democracy. This resiliency stems in large part from a fluid and robust political marketplace where ideas and policies compete and are constantly weighed and measured by public opinion and tested in the crucible of elections. Just as the stock market sorts strong companies from weak ones, so too does this marketplace, over time, sort good policies from bad ones. Thus, what some might call the "messiness" of U.S. politics is not actually a bug of the system, but a feature.

Admittedly, this political marketplace has lately become distorted and perverted in America. Americans are increasingly siloed into echo chambers and information bubbles, receiving curated and highly editorialized news reinforcing preexisting beliefs, instead of being exposed to alternative viewpoints and information that may challenge those beliefs. And with the advent of cancel culture in America, even expressing a contrary opinion or viewpoint can result in being demonized or censored. Misinformation and conspiracy theories perpetuate and gain traction through the internet and social media, radicalizing many Americans. This has led to Americans residing in very different worlds and operating under an uncommon set of facts and beliefs, making any true and honest debate of the issues of the day extremely difficult, even dangerous. This must change, beginning with prudent reform and regulation of big tech and social media companies, which bear a great deal of responsibility for these circumstances. If this does not occur, America will lose one of its greatest advantages, and democracy will suffer egregiously, as indeed it has already begun to do.

While the Founders sought to limit government, they also recognized proper roles for it, and that it must possess the requisite powers to adequately fulfill those roles. Namely, the goal of government was to secure and safeguard individual inalienable rights—life, liberty, and the pursuit of happiness—and create optimum conditions for free society and enterprise to thrive. This meant a government empowered to provide for the nation's defense, enforce the rule of law, engage in foreign policy, and preserve property and contractual rights. It also meant a government capable of building the nation's infrastructure and providing citizens with educational opportunities for advancement. By creating a limited government, with limited yet sufficient powers, the Founders intended government to focus on those delineated responsibilities, and not veer into other areas for which it was not empowered. For the Founders understood, as President Reagan astutely observed, that big government is not necessarily better government. Involvement in too many areas stretches resources thin while taking tax dollars more productively spent and invested by private individuals in the economy.

Of course, not all Americans now subscribe to the limitations placed upon their government by the Founders. For though the system worked incredibly well for centuries, turning America, and its form of government, into the envy of and model for the rest of the world, America is currently engaged in a heated dispute on whether and to what extent this form of government should continue. Debates of this sort have occurred periodically throughout U.S. history, with government changing over the years, especially in reaction to seismic events. In response to the Great Depression came FDR's New Deal reforms, pushing government into areas it had never been before, followed by President Lyndon B. Johnson's Great Society, which pushed government even further in the name of eliminating poverty and racial injustice. Then, sensing that government had gone too far, President Reagan ushered in a conservative revolution to make it smaller again.

America has arrived at yet another turning point in this regard following a tumultuous couple of decades that have included massive changes wrought by globalization and technology, the tragic events of 9/11, the financial crisis, the potential threat of climate change, and now the COVID-19 pandemic during which the government has acquired and employed unprecedented powers. As a result, many no longer desire a government of limited powers or even one constrained by the U.S. Constitution. Many desire instead a government involved to a significant degree in all aspects of American life and society, with powers exceeding anything the Founders ever envisioned. Some even desire to remake or re-found America completely, creating a government in their view more suited to the modern era.

This book is about the New Cold War, and though it will inevitably touch upon the role of government within that context, the scope of this book is not permissive of an extensive philosophical debate on government itself. Personally, I believe in a more limited government as designed by the Founders, but also one possessing powers necessary to win a war. And in the New Cold War, as in previous wars, the U.S. government must act in ways it would not in peace time, including becoming more active in certain areas of the economy, for example by ensuring that vital industries and technologies are made in America. What is critically important, however, is that while Americans debate the role of government, in the process America must not sacrifice the very advantages that have made it great in the first place. And indeed, many of the prescriptions in this book for victory in the New Cold War involve harnessing and leveraging those very advantages. Losing them would be catastrophic for America.

In his masterwork *The Republic,* the ancient Athenian philosopher Plato contended that democracies inevitably degenerate into anarchy, with the interests of the poor becoming adversarial to those of the rich, and the majority to those of the minority, and vice versa, leading to mob rule, and ultimately to tyranny. To avoid this fate, the Founders designed the U.S. political system with safeguards, including separation of powers and checks and balances so that no single individual, special interest, or branch of government could accrue and wield too much power. They also emphasized the importance of educating the American people on civics, democracy, and patriotism. Lately, though, these safeguards have fallen short, and are unable to tame or restrain the increasingly enflamed divisions and distortions of modern-day American politics. As a result, Plato's prophecy of anarchy and mob rule has grown significantly in America.

At the very end of first Cold War, as he set about implementing the reforms that would ultimately serve to dissolve the Soviet Union, Soviet President Mikhail Gorbachev is said to have famously remarked, referring to America: "We're going to do something terrible to you. We're going to deprive you of an enemy." His words proved prescient. For without the threat of a true rival, America has become embroiled in increasingly hostile internal conflicts, making enemies of fellow Americans as partisan divisions run rampant. And though the Founders repeatedly warned of the dangers of party factionalism, with President George Washington doing so explicitly in his farewell address, the dangers of factionalism have lately come to pass in America.

The U.S. political system is a two-party system, with the Republican Party and Democratic Party duking it out year after year, election after election, for power. In the past, the two parties held at least broad fundamental agreements about the country.

Now even that is no longer the case. And while there have always been strong disagreements between them, the parties have grown to despise one another, viewing each other not as fellow Americans unified in a common destiny, but as enemies to be defeated. These divisions have weakened America and pose a major lability in the New Cold War.

Exacerbating and enflaming these divisions further are class, identity, and racial politics. The last of these is particularly problematic for a racially diverse nation like America. Undoubtedly, given America's fraught history with race relations, especially relating to African Americans, race-related issues requiring resolution still exist. These may always exist to a degree due to the horrors of slavery. However, certain politicians have stoked these historical tensions for personal advancement, causing many occurrences, justified and otherwise, to be blown out of proportion. Other events that should provoke broad agreement or condemnation are polarized along political lines. This has enflamed race relations to levels reminiscent of the tumultuous days of the Civil Rights Era, something that has not gone unnoticed by America's enemies, who have sought to use it to their advantage.

Though America must of course recognize and rectify legitimate racial injustices, not everything can or should be seen through the lens of race and racism. Diversity can be a strength for America. But it can also be an Achilles heel if used to divide and pit one group of people against another. Going forward, Americans must decide once and for all whether they are one united American people, or whether they will continue allowing themselves to be balkanized by race and identity politics.

Regardless of partisan differences in other areas, for America to prevail in the New Cold War, there simply cannot be division on the China threat and what is required to counter it. There is hope in this regard, as a growing bipartisan consensus on China appears to be emerging, following a hardening of the public's mood on China stemming from the COVID-19 pandemic. It is one thing, though, to recognize the threat, and another entirely to possess the political willpower to enact measures necessary to combat it. Especially as the China threat demands a whole government approach, as will be discussed throughout this book. Difficult political choices on the economy, immigration, and education, among others, will need to be made. These choices will be unpopular with certain constituencies, and will engender strong opposition from industry groups, activists, and those disproportionately benefiting from the existing system. But to defeat China, these changes must be implemented. The CCP fears China becoming an area of agreement between Republicans and Democrats. Americans would do well to see these fears come to fruition.

Lee Kuan Yew contended that lack of compensation for those in government would lead to incompetent government. But in America a larger issue perhaps is the obscene amounts of money in politics. A congressional campaign alone now costs millions of dollars. This severely limits the pool of potential people who can and do run for elected office. And even while in office, elected officials spend an inordinate amount of their time and focus raising funds for their next campaign, rather than governing or legislating. Having to raise such enormous funds also transfers significant power to donors with the means of providing them, giving a small and select number of people and organizations disproportionate power over the entire system, distorting the system by effectively cornering it.

This also gives China, and by extension the CCP, significant influence over U.S. democracy by enabling China to commandeer U.S. corporations doing business in China to serve as their proxies in Washington. And through their large campaign donations, the CCP effectively purchases U.S. politicians to advocate for policies advantageous to China and detrimental to America. This represents a significant flaw and weakness in the U.S. political system. Addressing money in politics will not be an easy fix, but it will be a necessary one for the long-term health of U.S. democracy, and ultimately for America's ability to combat China. A prudent start in this regard would be banning companies doing business with China from making political donations.

Finally, any system of government, whether democracy or autocracy, will fail without strong, smart, patriotic people to lead it. And where once America attracted its strongest and most accomplished to serve their country in government, the quality of those in and running for elected office has declined precipitously. As a result, the American people continue to lose faith in and respect for their government and for those serving in it, with Congress alone currently holding a job approval rating of less than 20%.[36] It is essential that America once again attract its best and brightest to run for and serve in office. The American Republic depends upon it.

As discussed in this chapter, China and America possess certain advantages and disadvantages in their respective systems of government in the New Cold War. Both also face serious threats and challenges that may serve to strain their systems and impair their ability to fight and win. For America, it is political and racial divisions; for China, challenges to its autocratic rule and the bargain underpinning it. The political system better able to leverage its strengths while mitigating or eliminating its weaknesses will have the advantage. And like the first Cold War, that may ultimately determine which nation is victorious.

PART II

Know Thyself: America

CHAPTER 4
AN INDUSTRIAL STRATEGY FOR VICTORY

"The foundation of war is economics." – Elon Musk,
in relation to China overtaking America as the world's
largest economy

"Defense is of much more importance than opulence."
– Adam Smith, *Wealth of Nations*

Adam Smith, father of free trade and capitalism, wrote the above quote in *Wealth of Nations* in relation to the Navigation Acts of the 1600s, a series of laws restricting colonial trade to protect Britain's strategically important shipping industry, which would play a critical role in conflicts with other European powers. Smith, certainly no protectionist, acknowledged that although free trade was his preferred pathway to prosperity, it must take a backseat on occasion to national defense. Smith also understood battlefields to be markets and commerce as much as land and seas. History is littered with empires crumbling not from guns and bombs but from sheer economics.

China has learned this lesson well, just as America seems to have forgotten it. China views commerce and trade through the lens of national strength and security. As such, China exacts a significant price for foreigners to even access its market, including the transfer of technology, ultimately used to advance its own companies and military. Nor does China want foreigners dominating its market, or foreign competitors enriched. It wants its own companies to win and does everything possible to make it so, while America takes a more laissez faire approach to its own.

America even treats its greatest companies in an adversarial fashion, advocating that instead of building them up, they should be cut down to size. Perhaps this is because so many have changed their view on loyalty to America. It was once said that what was good for America was good for General Motors, and vice versa, meaning that the success of the country and the company were linked. They succeeded and prospered together. Since the onset of globalization, however, this has not been the case. U.S. corporations increasingly do not even view themselves as American, but instead as global citizens, belonging and loyal to no single country.

Chinese companies, by contrast, remain completely loyal to China. Of course, many are state-owned, or state controlled, and nearly all have CCP presence in their executive ranks. But Chinese companies are ultimately intended to serve China, not the other way around. And China would never have allowed its companies to outsource Chinese jobs to other countries the way America has. Even if it meant increased profits for a company or a sector, China knew the loss of Chinese jobs would be detrimental to social cohesion and ultimately sap overall national strength, conferring a short-term gain in return for a far larger long-term loss. America's experience bears this out. And far from hindering its global competitiveness, China now boasts some of the strongest companies in the world. Alibaba, Tencent, Lenovo and Huawei, just to name a few, are all global leaders.

And while the U.S. government allows U.S. companies to compete freely and fairly against foreign companies in the global economy, China's government not only creates and builds Chinese national champion companies but also provides them with every advantage possible to conquer global markets, including massive amounts of financial support and subsidies. This is the equivalent of a sports team giving its best players steroids. As a result, American companies are competing on an increasingly unlevel playing field decidedly rigged in China's favor, for they are not only competing with Chinese companies for global markets, but also with the entire Chinese government.

That is not to say that China's brand of state-driven capitalism has not bred inefficiencies and weaknesses. Indeed, it has, one being staggering amounts of non-performing investment and debt. But so far, these weaknesses have not impeded China on its march towards overtaking America economically. To the contrary, far from exploiting China's weaknesses, America has allowed China to rise by taking advantage of America's own economic vulnerabilities, including America's adherence to free and open markets.

To combat China, America must rethink how it evaluates national economic strength. It must look beyond such measures as GDP growth, and instead think about the economy from a strategic standpoint, with an eye towards great power competition with China. America must ask what it means for an economy to be strategically strong and resilient. For example, if critical supply chains such as medicine and medical supplies are controlled by China, can America truly say it is economically strong? Posed another way, would America have allowed the Soviet Union to control such important supply chains during the Cold War? Of course not. Neither should America allow China to—regardless of whether individual U.S. companies may profit. As Adam Smith said, defense takes priority. And whatever short-term profit is gained, America will pay dearly later.

There will surely be those denouncing this as economic protectionism. I wonder whether the same people would not protect U.S. military installations in a war. For industries and companies are akin to military installations in the New Cold War. That is how China views them. America must therefore ensure their protection, just as it would military installations, and begin to think of economic security as national security. In short, America must build an economy to withstand and win a war.

To begin with, the U.S. must coldly evaluate and assess its economy based on potential war with China, including which industries will be the most strategically important; what supplies, goods and materials the U.S. must be able to manufacture and produce; what supply chain weaknesses China will target, and how the U.S. can turn those weaknesses into strengths. It will also require the U.S. to leverage all means and resources at its disposal to ensure U.S. companies possess every competitive economic advantage, especially in strategically important industries. As Sun Tzu said:

> "The art of war teaches us to rely not on the likelihood of the enemy's not coming, but on our own readiness to receive him; not on the chance of his not attacking, but rather on the fact that we have made our position unassailable."

This requires America to adjust its views of the free market system. Simply relying upon the market for economic security is a fool's errand, for the free market and its participants seek profit, not national security. Unlike a market, a nation has goals beyond sheer maximization of profit. It does not make sense to resign the nation's economic security to the vicissitudes of the market. America needs a mentality shift, one that places national interest above pure economic interest, or better yet, views them as one and the same.

And indeed, America has fully understood and practiced this for much of its history. It is in fact in large part what allowed America to become a rich and powerful nation in the first place. As Clyde Prestowitz persuasively details in his book, *The World Turned Upside Down: America, China, and the Struggle for Global Leadership*, America rose and became the world's richest and most powerful nation not through embracing free trade and open markets, as erroneously believed, but through active government protection, enhancement, and development of key American industries alongside mercantilist trade policies. Ironically, China is copying the very formula America utilized to rise to power, while America in turn has abandoned it, just as before, the British abandoned the formula while America learned it and quickly overtook them. America must relearn its own history and rediscover its economic roots before it is too late, and history repeats itself with China overtaking America as America once did the British.

That is not to say America should cease being capitalist or embracing market forces. America has succeeded and prospered tremendously from both. Nor can government create jobs, innovation, or wage growth as effectively as the private sector. Government cannot supplant private enterprise in powering an economy. Even communist China came to that realization. But over the last few decades, America has placed blind faith in the market, trusting that it will always do what is in America's best interest. China has exploited this to its advantage. Going forward, America must take a more nuanced view of the market, particularly as it relates to strategically important sectors. It must continue to utilize the market to obtain its great benefits, such as growth and innovation, but cannot allow the market to simply dictate outcomes. Too much is at stake.

This does not mean that America should adopt a state-centric system like China. It does however mean that America must once again become comfortable with the state taking a more active role in terms of driving commercial investment. It also means embracing a more patriotic form of capitalism, which continues to harness the power, growth, competition, and creativity of the market, while simultaneously ensuring that it is directed towards and in alignment with national strategic interests, for example by ensuring that vital supply chains and industries remain in America, and that U.S. workers are prioritized over foreign ones. It also means corporations and government working together in partnership to ensure that America, not China, wins critical technologies and industries of the future.

To that end, America needs a coherent national economic strategy with a pro-American industrial policy at its center. A long-term economic blueprint for the nation can identify economic sectors vital to the national interest and how to help them thrive in America. The goal should not be to restrain or curtail private enterprise in any way but instead to harness and drive it towards outcomes vital to the national interest, which markets alone cannot achieve. This would create the conditions which will allow America to unleash what in World War II President Franklin Roosevelt called "The Arsenal of Democracy."

U.S. Industrial Policy

Some will cringe when they hear the term "industrial policy," as it conjures visions of Soviet style five-year plans. But industrial policies have a rich history in America, including FDR's Arsenal of Democracy, Alexander Hamilton's Report on Manufactures and Henry Clay's American System, which was strongly supported by Abraham Lincoln. And as pointed out by Robert D. Atkinson and Stephen J. Ezell in their book *Innovation Economics: The Race for*

Global Advantage, even the great government skeptic President Ronald Reagan advocated for and adopted a national U.S. industrial policy aimed at competing directly with both the Soviet Union and Japan. Likewise, America now needs a new industrial policy aimed at competing directly with China.

The U.S. industrial policy should not be about picking winners or losers, but instead about encouraging and boosting sectors vital to America's strategic interests, which will determine global leadership. This should be done in ways that further America's competitive advantages, while also correcting or supplementing areas not adequately addressed through the market. The industrial policy should not attempt to supplant private enterprise in favor of government, or have government dictate to industry how business should be run. Rather, America's industrial policy should complement and enhance private enterprise. Ultimately, it is about choosing America and its workers over other nations, fostering innovation, and giving the U.S. every competitive economic advantage possible to win the New Cold War against China.

America already makes choices and subsidizes certain industries, favoring some over others, while influencing all kinds of economic activities through the tax code. For example, America encourages homeownership through the mortgage tax deduction. But this is often done in a non-strategic, even ad hoc fashion that accrues to entrenched and politically powerful interests, furthering crony capitalism and rent-seeking behavior, as large, well-connected businesses successfully lobby government to protect their interests from competition or, in many cases, even innovation. This has the effect of stifling America's dynamism and ability to adapt to changing global trends and technologies. A strategic industrial policy can change this by ensuring investment flows where it is most needed, rather than to the most politically connected.

To facilitate the U.S. industrial policy and safeguard it from being highjacked by political and special interests, becoming yet another political slush fund, benefiting politically connected individuals and companies and funding partisan political priorities instead of strategically important ones, a National Industrial Commission should be established. The Commission should be comprised of the brightest minds from the business, military, science, and technology sectors, and include leaders responsible for actual goods, infrastructure, services, and defense. It should also be independent to remain un-swayed by political vicissitudes and focus objectively on the strategic economic interests of the nation. Moreover, the Commission should not only be responsible for crafting and overseeing the U.S. industrial policy but also for ensuring its success, with powers requisite to the task.

In essence, the Commission should become akin to a modern-day version of the War Production Board (WPB) established by FDR and utilized to great effect by America during World War II to defeat Nazi Germany. Like the WPB, the Commission should evaluate America's strategic economic needs and determine which industries and supply chains must be prioritized and enhanced to win the New Cold War. The Commission should also be fully empowered to accomplish the goals of the industrial policy, including the ability to cut through red tape to expedite important projects and technologies. This will not only circumvent potential regulatory bias but also be critically important in the fast-moving high-tech competition with China. Burdensome regulations and bureaucratic processes must not be allowed to impede America's ability to compete and win. An empowered Commission will ensure they do not.

Importantly, the industrial policy cannot and should not be accomplished simply through large additional amounts of government spending, but instead through incentivizing and partnering with private enterprise. New and creative public-private partnerships therefore must be explored and formed to accomplish national economic goals. The U.S. must also examine existing government funding and subsidies currently going to industries and interests not in alignment with national industrial policies and repurpose them to those in alignment. This includes closing tax loopholes and other distortions and using those revenues to boost strategic sectors. The U.S. must also engage in the serious reform of entitlement spending, which is squeezing out funding necessary to accomplish national economic goals. Not only will the U.S. and taxpayers save money by reducing entitlement spending, while increasing spending for education, transportation, and scientific research and development, but also, this will ultimately generate greater tax revenue through stimulation of the economy. Thus, if implemented correctly, the U.S. industrial policy should be cost neutral or better in the long run, while significantly boosting the economy and America's competitiveness, and providing higher paying jobs for American workers.

Broadly speaking, the goals of the U.S. industrial policy should be three-fold: 1. identifying, protecting, and enhancing strategically important industries, sectors, and technologies and ensuring they thrive in America; 2. reshoring and securing vital supply chains in America; and 3. promoting and protecting American workers and American jobs.

The tools to accomplish these goals should be broad and myriad. They should also be, wherever possible, incentive-based. Charlie Munger, Warren Buffett's long-time business partner famously once said, "show me the incentive and I will show you the outcome." Like humans generally, market participants respond to incentives and disincentives; or, put another way, carrots and sticks. And to ensure pro-American economic outcomes, a mixture of incentives and disincentives should be employed to adjust the market's behavior towards those outcomes.

For instance, special tax credits should be provided to strategic industries that determine global leadership, along with full expensing of certain expenditures, including for research and development. The U.S. government should also follow Japan's lead and utilize direct subsidies to pay companies to reshore production. This can be accomplished, in part, by significantly reducing or waiving corporate taxes for repatriation of overseas profits. Tax cuts and credits should also be tied to locating facilities in America and hiring U.S. workers, while imposing punitive taxes on U.S. companies that outsource U.S. jobs. Additional punitive measures for outsourcing companies should include being barred from accessing taxpayer funding or financing, and curtailment of the ability to transfer data through data privacy laws. These actions will not only serve to level the playing field by taking away competitive cost advantages of outsourcing, but also make it more advantageous and profitable to hire U.S. workers.

Furthermore, as a huge consumer of goods and services, government has enormous power to affect market behavior and drive commercial investment, for example, through its procurement policies. By making policies regarding its business partners and practices, government directly influences market behavior. To incentivize companies to align with pro-American policies, especially in targeted industries, government should be required to contract with U.S. based companies that hire U.S. workers and produce products in America. Strengthening and expanding existing legislation like the Buy American Act would present a good start in this regard. Federal pension and public investment funds should also be required to invest in America and American companies, whether exclusively or at a very high percentage.

Along with providing incentives in strategic industries, government must also play a nurturing role in nascent or "infant" industries and emerging technologies that may not be commercially viable by not only helping to fund them but also by providing demand that does not yet exist. This is especially important as U.S. companies have significantly reduced their R & D budgets and spending. And due to the short termism inherent in public markets, companies are deterred from making huge investments and taking uncertain risks on new technologies that may not be commercially viable for many years, if ever. This fact, coupled with an overall reduction in U.S. government spending on scientific R & D, has caused the U.S. to lose its one unrivaled innovation advantage. This comes at a time when China is pouring enormous resources into R & D and racing ahead to replace America as the world's innovation leader. America cannot allow China to win this race, for to do so means the industries and inventions of the future will be made in China, not America, a result with profound consequences in the New Cold War and for America's future and prosperity.

In the past, America has benefited tremendously by seeding new industries before they became commercially viable. Notable examples include the internet, global positioning systems, and artificial intelligence, all of which continue to pay enormous dividends. Along with supplying grants and government research and development funding, government should facilitate strategic partnerships in these industries between companies, universities, and government to create conducive ecosystems for these industries to thrive in America and quickly build economies of scale. This will accelerate much needed investment into these industries and not only help establish players in the targeted industries, but also cause others to enter them, creating greater competition and investment. Talented individuals will in turn find these industries more attractive, and colleges and universities will respond by enhancing requisite academic departments, creating a virtuous cycle. Indeed, famous innovation and tech hubs like Silicon Valley in California and the Research Triangle in North Carolina were created in a similar manner.

Further, America should create an investment fund, let us call it the Patriot Fund, to invest in and alongside private capital in promising industries, emerging technologies, and in what some call "unicorn" companies. The Patriot Fund would be akin to a national venture capital or sovereign wealth fund. And indeed, many countries, including China, already have funds of this nature which are investing massive amounts of capital into companies, markets, industries, and technologies. These funds not only create wealth for their countries and their citizens but also allow them to gain stakes in strategically important technologies and companies while moving and creating entirely new markets and industries. America cannot afford not to have a similar fund of its own, from either a financial or a geopolitical perspective, or America and its companies will be at a strategic disadvantage to China and other countries that do have them.

In addition to helping America from a strategic standpoint, the Patriot Fund could also serve to enhance the lives and financial wellbeing of the American people, with shares of the fund even issued directly to the American people across all income classes, so that they have a direct financial stake and broadly benefit from the wealth of the nation. This can also be a way to satisfy growing calls for the provision of basic income and other forms of government-provided financial security. This will assist in enhancing much needed social cohesion and help the American people buy into the goals of the U.S. industrial policy by having a direct stake in its success. By doing so, the American people can even be enlisted to help accomplish the goals of the U.S. industrial policy. For example, as consumers, the American people can exert tremendous influence on companies to align with pro-America industrial policies and drive economic behavior generally towards a more patriotic capitalism.

Additionally, the industrial policy should help reallocate labor and connect Americans to in-demand jobs in promising industries of the future. The COVID-19 pandemic has provided an enormous opportunity in this respect, with many people, especially those in service and travel related sectors, laid off and facing an uncertain future. The industrial policy should assist in getting these people re-skilled and into emerging industries. To that end, America must implement a complementary national education strategy, which will be discussed at length later in this book. Government should also coordinate with and empower labor unions, chambers of commerce, and trade associations to assist in this endeavor.

Individual U.S. states should be incentivized to fulfill the goals of the U.S. industrial policy. Federal aid and grant money should even be conditioned upon meeting national economic strategic objectives. States will in turn incentivize their local governments and market participants to fulfill them, and so it will trickle down and filter throughout the entire economic system. States will also compete to lure in strategic industries to take advantage of the federal incentives, adding an extra level of competition to boost strategic sectors. And as the "laboratories of democracy," states can experiment with creative approaches that if successful can be exported to other states and even adopted nationally.

In certain cases involving industries and supply lines of the greatest strategic importance, the U.S. must go beyond incentives and disincentives. In these cases, the Defense Production Act should be invoked to force companies to return critical supply chains to America. Recently, former President Trump used the Act to speed U.S. production of medical supplies amid the COVID-19 pandemic, and subsequently to speed development of mines of strategically important rare earths vital to new and existing technologies.

Use of the Act should be expanded to other essential industries and supply chains as well.

Manufacturing

It is imperative for overall national strength, resiliency, and security that U.S. manufacturing is revitalized. Bluntly stated, America must be able to make things again, and must fully invest in doing so. Indeed, what value is innovation when the goods and products stemming from it are ultimately built somewhere else? And without manufacturing, America can never truly be economically strong and resilient. Nor will America ever be able to overcome its over-reliance on imported goods and decrease its massive trade deficit with China, which itself represents a strategic liability in the New Cold War. Losing manufacturing to China and other low-cost labor countries was one of America's single biggest mistakes. It is in fact a primary reason for China's rise and America's decline.

Not only has America lost entire manufacturing industries across the value chain, even ones they once dominated, but also, it has lost entire skill sets. Indeed, at this point America can barely even make the most basic goods such as clothing or appliances domestically, leaving it highly vulnerable during a disaster or national emergency. For example, during the COVID-19 pandemic, America struggled mightily to even produce simple masks and other medical supplies for its citizens and was forced to import them from, among other places, China. This is simply unacceptable and cannot continue. This grave mistake must be rectified whatever the costs. Manufacturing must therefore be the heart of the U.S. industrial policy.

America cannot compete in low-cost labor manufacturing with China, a country of 1.4 billion people that pays its workers far less than America, or indeed most of the world. This is a losing battle for America, and a competitive advantage for China. In fact, even

China is losing low-cost manufacturing to even lower cost labor countries like Vietnam. America cannot and should not engage in a low-cost labor race to the bottom. That does not mean, however, that America cannot compete and win again in manufacturing.

As part of its industrial policy, America must invest heavily in robotics and automation to bring back a strong U.S. manufacturing sector that can win globally while creating jobs not existing currently. Automation should not be feared but fully embraced by America. It may cause job losses and disruption in the near term—something which certainly needs to be accounted for and addressed—but it will also create far more new jobs and opportunities in the long term, as technology has throughout history. Moreover, the rise of machines will not so much substitute humans as complement them by supplementing and enhancing skill sets. Workers who become adept at working with automation and robotics will continue to improve and find new and innovative ways to create even greater progress. America once possessed the most skilled manufacturing workers in the world, and by fully embracing automation, it can do so again.

To further increase U.S. manufacturing competitiveness internationally, and by doing so bring back manufacturing domestically, America should strategically devalue the U.S. dollar. Not only will this make U.S. goods more competitive in overseas markets but also it will increase prices for imported goods in America, such as those from China, ultimately causing the growth in demand for imports to slow. This will have the effect of strongly encouraging U.S. consumers to switch to domestically produced goods, providing support for and catalyzing much needed investment in U.S. manufacturing. As an extra bonus, devaluing the dollar will detrimentally affect China's economy, which remains heavily reliant on cheap exports. By increasing the Chinese currency relative to the dollar, and thus decreasing the competitiveness of Chinese goods in international markets, demand for Chinese exports will fall. Indeed, this is the very strategy China successfully pursued against America to build up its own manufacturing sector and weaken America's. It is high time America repaid them in kind.

In conjunction with strategic currency intervention, America should boost domestic manufacturing through the implementation of border adjustment taxes, just as many other countries do. Under a border-adjusted tax (BAT), American goods and services sold overseas would be free of the U.S. tax, while sales of imported goods and services made elsewhere would be subject to the U.S. tax. This would make imports more expensive, while supporting American exports. BAT would discourage U.S. companies from producing products in foreign low-tax countries and then selling them to U.S. consumers, or purchasing cheaper parts from other countries. BAT would also force foreign companies selling goods in America to build factories and plants in America. This would ultimately mean more American jobs and would produce significant tax revenue which can be utilized to provide tax and other financial incentives to American manufacturers.

Infrastructure

Along with manufacturing, America must address and invest in internal improvements as part of its industrial policy to build the infrastructure of the future.

Currently, America's infrastructure is crumbling and falling woefully behind, just as China is building new cities seemingly overnight. Infrastructure is crucially important for America's overall economic strength and resiliency. Building infrastructure on a grand scale will enhance productivity throughout the economy while employing thousands of U.S. workers and companies. As such, America must invest in an ambitious infrastructure program, which should include 5G digital infrastructure, roads, bridges, and highspeed rail.

To facilitate and fund this infrastructure program, America should create a national infrastructure bank which can leverage public and private funding to provide low-cost financing to support critical infrastructure projects throughout the nation. Other advanced nations, like the United Kingdom, are already establishing similar infrastructure banks, and America should follow suit.[37]

The U.S. should explore other potential infrastructure funding sources as well. This could include imposing a surcharge on certain foreign investment into the U.S., the proceeds from which would go towards funding infrastructure. Additionally, an impact fee could be tied to immigration. Whereby, new immigrants would pay a certain proportionate sum, either upon entry to America or over a specified period of time, which would go to funding infrastructure. This would be fair and reasonable, as new immigrants utilize existing U.S. infrastructure while necessitating the building of additional infrastructure. It would also provide Americans with a direct upfront benefit from immigration, making immigration overall more attractive.

Trade

As part of, and in conjunction with its industrial policy, America must address trade, and ensure that to the extent possible it furthers America's economic and strategic interests.

Trade and trade agreements in and of themselves are not bad. Indeed, they can be very good. But trade must be managed. And as discussed, U.S. workers have been badly hurt by trade since China entered the WTO. Thankfully, America has at long last pushed back by erecting protective and reciprocal tariffs to balance the scales. But

America must go further still to rectify and combat China's numerous trade abuses, including reassessing the terms of its membership in the WTO, which has forced America to follow certain rules while allowing China to play by another set. It is long past time that America, along with other WTO countries, demand reform to stop China's trade abuses, including the absurdity of China being a "developing country." America should also engage in strategic trade through mutually beneficial trade agreements with ally nations, especially those strategically disadvantageous to China. America will find willing partners in this regard in the EU and Pacific Rim nations, such as Japan, Australia, and South Korea, who are particularly weary of China and its malign economic power and influence.

While America engages in mutually beneficial trade, however, it must also protect its strategic industries, as other nations do. America recognized this from its earliest days, as strongly advocated by, among others, Alexander Hamilton. Funds from tariffs should therefore be re-invested back into U.S. industries, so as to not only protect strategically important industries but also strengthen them. In return, government must ensure that industries and companies are not simply surviving by being protected from competition. Government cannot become a blank check or safety net for industry. Instead, protection must come with conditions and metrics to ensure that industry can compete successfully and ultimately stand and win on its own.

In addition to developing new tools, existing U.S. trade programs and agencies should also be fully employed, funded, and leveraged to help America win in trade. One such being the U.S. Export-Import Bank (EXIM), which can not only help significantly enhance U.S. trade, but advance U.S. geopolitical goals as well.

EXIM is America's official export credit agency (ECA), and it facilitates trade between U.S. domestic exporters and foreign buyers.

EXIM helps foreign countries, and their companies, buy American made goods and services. EXIM provides competitive loans and other forms of financing to foreign entities for the purpose of purchasing goods and services produced by America. This is especially important when dealing with developing markets. Through EXIM, America can significantly boost U.S. exports to emerging market countries, which will open up enormous economic opportunities for U.S. companies, while also helping America to build strong relationships in these countries, and by doing so, counter China's influence in them. As such, it is imperative not only from a trade perspective, but also a geopolitical one, that EXIM be sufficiently funded and empowered to help America win the New Cold War.

Above all, it is critically important that America continues to foster and further its great entrepreneurial and optimistic culture, the distinct American culture that built the greatest nation and economy in the world. The U.S. must continue to give people wide freedom to create and innovate, and encourage economic pioneering and risk taking. It must support its entrepreneurs and innovators, even hold them up as heroes to be celebrated and emulated. For in the New Cold War against China, they will be as integral to victory as military soldiers have been in previous wars.

Finally, America must once again do big things and believe it can. The industrial policy can help in this respect by creating a sense of national purpose, and should be given all the marketing power necessary to inspire the nation to achieve economic greatness.

CHAPTER 5

A NEW NATIONAL DEFENSE
EDUCATION ACT

*"Our progress as a nation can be no swifter than our progress
in education. The human mind is our fundamental resource."*
– President John F. Kennedy

*"Upon the education of the people of this country the fate of
this country depends."* – Benjamin Disraeli

At the onset of the first Cold War, the U.S. educational system was in crisis, and U.S. students were woefully lagging behind their European counterparts. It took the shock to national pride of Sputnik to spark significant educational reform. President Eisenhower pushed for and Congress enacted the National Defense Education Act (NDEA) of 1958 to promote and finance education in science and technology in the name of national security. Under the NDEA, the U.S. government invested heavily in developing a new curriculum suited to winning the Cold War, including greatly expanding math and science programs. The effects of NDEA were revolutionary. Not only did it help the U.S. win the Cold War by cultivating a domestic supply of mathematicians and scientists, but it also paid dividends well into the future, including by laying the foundation for America's computer and dot-com revolutions of the 1980s and 1990s.[38]

Over the last two decades, however, America has fallen behind in STEM subjects: science, technology, engineering, and mathematics. Once the best in the world, the U.S. education system is now failing far too often in far too many places. It is also a system built for another time, and increasingly outdated and unsuited for the modern high-tech world. While the U.S. slips in its once unrivalled scientific leadership, China is pouring enormous resources into STEM education, and now leads the world in the number of STEM graduates.

So it is that at the start of the New Cold War, America finds itself in a similar position to where it was at the start of the first Cold War. And just as America needs a new national economic strategy, it also needs a corresponding and complementary national education strategy. As President Eisenhower correctly observed, the two are linked. The education system will determine whether America leads in critical strategic fields and industries of the future or falls behind China and other countries.

To begin with, not all subjects are or should be treated equally in the new high-tech world. It is imperative that STEM education be prioritized with corresponding resources devoted to the STEM disciplines which will determine future world leadership. STEM prioritization must begin as early as possible, for by the time students reach the university level, it is too late. This issue is reflected in the fact that foreign students, many of whom come from China, currently comprise most of the undergraduate and graduate student population in STEM disciplines in American universities. And while the rest of the world, including China, prioritizes STEM education, U.S. student engagement in STEM is fading. Tech companies in Silicon Valley already claim that without foreign nationals, they would be unable to fill the gaps in their ranks. America must reverse this trend immediately, and must cultivate a strong domestic supply of STEM students and graduates. The importance of this cannot be overstated.

The New Cold War will be a tech war, a race for supremacy in the technologies and industries of the future, like artificial intelligence, 5G, clean energy, and quantum computing. The front-line soldiers will be STEM field workers. China understands this and views the creation of domestic STEM talent akin to building military capabilities in the New Cold War. China has poured enormous resources into STEM and is producing more STEM graduates every year. Chinese STEM graduates not only come from China's domestic universities but also often hail from top U.S. universities. In fact, China sends more students to U.S. universities than any other country.[39] In many ways, the U.S. is educating and training the very individuals China is using to wage war against it.

The U.S. must view its top research and science universities as strategic assets and treat them as such. This includes ensuring that they are not used by China to develop STEM talent and steal critical technology and research through its Thousand Talents Program, and others like it. The U.S. government must also do everything within its power to encourage and incentivize U.S. students to enter STEM disciplines. This should include providing special scholarships for students majoring in STEM disciplines and waiving or forgiving student loan debt for those entering STEM fields. The U.S. government should also ensure that its universities prioritize U.S. students in STEM disciplines over foreign ones. University funding should even be conditioned upon scholarships for U.S. students entering STEM majors.

Furthermore, the U.S. government must provide additional funding for teachers in STEM disciplines. Great STEM teachers are imperative to inspiring and creating legions of STEM students. This is true not only at the university level, but also at the earliest stages of education. STEM teachers must be thought of differently, including in terms of how they are trained. America requires STEM teachers who understand and can teach future technologies in a high-tech environment. Requirements for STEM teaching degrees and related certificates therefore must be reassessed. Training should include requiring continuing education so that STEM teachers are versed in the latest technologies. Ultimately, STEM teachers must be viewed as highly skilled workers themselves and should be compensated accordingly. Indeed, teaching generally must become a more elite profession in America, as it is in China, with great teachers properly incentivized and richly rewarded, and poor teachers quickly rooted out.

In addition to ensuring that traditional U.S. public schools have strong STEM programs, there must be a focus on STEM charter and specialty schools. School choice in STEM should be widely encouraged to create competition and to provide students opportunities that may not otherwise exist where they live. Public-private partnerships should be fully utilized to create STEM incubators and other STEM-related programs to assist local schools and neighborhoods in building strong STEM ecosystems. This should include businesses providing funding, equipment, and expertise to assist and encourage STEM students.

To maximize overall U.S. economic strength, education should be linked to employment and reflective of the labor needs of the nation. To accomplish this goal, the U.S. must guarantee to the extent possible that all its students possess skills necessary to thrive in the future high-tech world. This is particularly important as the real world becomes further integrated with robotics, artificial intelligence, and automation, making many existing jobs obsolete. To enhance competitiveness and social cohesion, the U.S. education system must adequately prepare its students for this new world. Otherwise, far too many people will be left behind, as is already the case.

Presently, the U.S. education system is not producing workers with the skills to meet the needs of the current and future labor market. U.S. employers constantly bemoan the mismatch in skills among workers, particularly acute when it comes to digital and technical skills. To a degree, technology will always be ahead of education, and therefore the skills needed for future technologies will also lag. But the gap must be closed to the extent possible. To do so, America must change its thinking on education generally, and who is responsible for it. Education must increasingly be a whole of society effort, a strategic partnership between business, education, community, and government.

Business has perhaps the greatest stake in the success of the education system, as the workforce directly determines its ability to grow and thrive. Companies are already spending heavily on education and training to upskill their workers. But business cannot simply be involved in education after workers are hired. It must do so at every level, from the earliest stages onward, especially in the economy of the future. Rapid technological progress will cause education and training to never truly end as workers are forced to upgrade skills continuously while learning new ones. It makes sense then that business be involved in the education system throughout to ensure that a proper foundation of in-demand skills are being taught. Not only will this help build a skilled workforce, but also, it will ultimately save significant costs.

An important way that business can and should involve itself in education is through school-to-work programs. America should fully embrace the dual training education model, combining classroom courses and hands-on experience, often through apprentice-ships in a company and vocational education. Germany has provided an excellent template to emulate in this regard, through its incredibly successful VET system. Other countries such as Austria, Switzerland, and South Korea have implemented similar systems. Dual education training can play a crucial role in bringing manufacturing back to America, as it has in these other countries.

To foster this system, government should incentivize companies to partner in dual education training by providing tax credits and other financial carrots for companies that sponsor apprenticeship-type programs. These programs will bring enormous benefits to both students and companies, as along with an expansion of vocational schools generally, apprenticeship programs will provide a much-needed avenue for individuals not drawn to or able to afford college. By helping America establish a respected nationwide vocational training system, business can alleviate stigmas associated with career and technical training, especially for those raised in the college or bust model. This will be instrumental in not only creating a skilled and prepared workforce, but also in helping many students obtain successful careers and utilize human resources otherwise not fully employed.

Just as business must assist the education system, the education system must in turn become more reflective of the real world. This includes updating the curriculum, which in the case of U.S. high schools has largely been unchanged for nearly a century, to reflect the demands of the modern world. To successfully compete with students in other countries and adequately prepare students for the real world, K through 12 schooling should also be year-round in America. Taking months off in the summer no longer makes sense, and countries around the world do not do it, putting U.S. students at a competitive disadvantage. It is an antiquated model from a time without widespread modern conveniences like air conditioning. It is also counterproductive. When kids leave school during the summer, they lose much of the learning obtained during the year, which then must be retaught when the next school year begins. This wastes valuable time far better spent on obtaining new skills and knowledge.

Another increasingly obsolete facet of the U.S. education system is its overemphasis on rote memorization and standardized testing. These learning practices are outdated in a world where knowledge and facts are only a Google search away. U.S. education should instead become interdisciplinary, with a concentration on fostering creativity, critical thinking, resourcefulness, and real-world problem solving. This will provide the U.S. with competitive advantages over China in the future, especially as the Chinese education system is extremely geared toward high stakes standardized testing and rote memorization, far more so even than America. China produces legions of Chinese students great at achieving high standardized test scores and excelling within controlled environments, but not in dynamic and unpredictable ones, like those in the real world. In the future, creativity, critical thinking, imagination, and the ability to innovate will be prized above all, for these are the sorts of skills at which computers and machines do not excel. U.S. students already lead Chinese students in these areas and this competitive advantage should continue to be fully leveraged and exploited.

The U.S. education system also cannot continue to be a rigid, inflexible, and largely one size fits all model. Like so much else in the modern age, it must increasingly be customized and tailored to each individual student. Far too many students are falling behind, or not realizing their fullest potential because they simply do not respond to the current system of teaching. The goal of the education system should not be to winnow good students from bad, but rather to ensure that students learn important skills allowing them to successfully compete in the job market. The current system does the opposite by implanting a competition to excel at certain kinds of learning to the exclusion of others that may be better for individual students and rewarding the acquisition of credentials over skills—perpetuating the college or bust model that has resulted in so much wasted talent and a shortage of critical skilled labor for employers. This must change. Along with a general refocus on skills, school choice can assist in this endeavor by allowing students to find schools and methods of learning that work best for them, increasing their chances for success.

This does not mean, however, that by being more flexible or accommodative that school should become easier or less rigorous. To the contrary, U.S. schools must continually raise the bar. They must become institutions relentlessly driven by the pursuit and achievement of excellence, with the highest academic standards in the world. It is only then that America can truly have again the world's best education system.

Finally, and in many ways most importantly, U.S. schools must teach civics and instill in students a strong sense of pride in their country. This is critically important for creating an informed and patriotic citizenry, and is particularly important for democracy. Unfortunately, far too many American students are coming out of U.S schools with a skewed and perverted view of America. This has profoundly negative effects on social cohesion and breeds divisiveness. It also leads to misinformation about America and its system of government. This can be extremely dangerous, particularly in the New Cold War, where sacrifices will need to be made, and China will do all it can to create fissures and divisions among the American public. Love of country and patriotism are antidotes to these tactics.

CHAPTER 6
IMMIGRATION FOR NATIONAL POWER

"I received a letter just before I left office from a man. I don't know why he chose to write it, but I'm glad he did. He wrote that you can go to live in France, but you can't become a Frenchman. You can go to live in Germany or Italy, but you can't become a German, an Italian. He went through Turkey, Greece, Japan and other countries. But he said anyone, from any corner of the world, can come to live in the United States and become an American." – President Ronald Reagan

"Demography is destiny." – Auguste Comte

The makeup of a nation's population is an important component of national power. In many ways, China and America have very different populations, particularly when it comes to immigration. China has a huge domestic population and very little immigration, while America possesses a smaller domestic population, relative to China, but has the highest proportion of immigrants among developed nations. In the context of the New Cold War, which provides the greater strategic advantage, a larger homogenous population with few immigrants, or a smaller diverse population with a high percentage of immigrants?

Singapore leader Lee Kuan Yew, once hailed by foreign policy experts as the wisest man in the East, argued that America had the advantage. He even predicted that China would not overtake America in the 21st century because China's culture would force it to rely on its domestic workforce. By contrast, America's openness to immigration meant it could draw the best and brightest from a diverse global talent pool of seven billion people.[40]

Lee Kuan Yew is certainly correct that immigration has conferred tremendous competitive advantages on America. Immigrants for example have been integral to the success of Silicon Valley, with more than a third of Silicon Valley tech workers foreign-born, including highly successful tech entrepreneurs like the late Steve Jobs and Elon Musk. And nearly half of recent U.S. Nobel Prize winners in STEM fields are immigrants.[41] Immigration has also enhanced U.S. influence throughout the world and helped the U.S. stave off demographic decline faced by other developed nations, including China.

Mass immigration, however, has also not been without significant costs to America, including the fraying of social cohesion, which has grown throughout the years. The U.S. immigration system went from tightly controlled to a veritable free for all, with millions of people entering the country illegally, or by exploiting gaping loopholes. This caused many Americans to sour on immigration all together, as their government appears unable to control the nation's borders or even determine who enters the country. Immigrants also compete with U.S. citizens, displacing jobs and lowering wages, a problem particularly acute in lower skilled jobs susceptible to low wage immigrant labor. Coupled with competition from low-cost labor in China, cheap immigrant labor has dealt a devastating blow to many U.S. workers. Low wage immigrant labor has also increased economic inequality in America by not only depressing wage rates for workers but also increasing the economic returns to capital disproportionately benefiting from low wage labor.

Thus, immigration has been both boon and burden for America, depending upon where one sits along the socioeconomic spectrum. Going forward, America must balance the legitimate benefits of immigration with the downsides, and, to the degree possible, emphasize the former while mitigating the latter. To do so, America must adopt immigration policies that enhance overall national strength and benefit the existing populace to the maximum extent. In this regard, America's current immigration policies have proven inadequate.

Like any sovereign nation, America has the absolute power and right to determine whether and to what extent it engages in immigration. And throughout its history, U.S. immigration policies have changed to either encourage or discourage immigration, or certain kinds of immigration. Generally, these changes reflected the needs of the country at the time, or the desires of the populace, or some combination of both. For example, in the 1800s, the U.S. had very open immigration policies intended to draw people to settle and populate America's wide-open lands. In the first half of the 1900s, in response to a large wave of mass immigration, the U.S. enacted restrictive policies to slow down immigration. Then in the second half of the century the immigration doors were largely thrown back open and have for the most part, barring a few slight changes here and there, stayed that way to date.

The time has come again for America to revisit its immigration policies to reflect its current and future strategic needs. This is imperative in the New Cold War, as immigration is not simply an economic issue, but a national security one as well. And if the first Cold War was an arms race for nuclear weapons, the New Cold War will be an arms race for talent, specifically talent relating to high-tech industries that will define global leadership.

China has a massive population, four times that of the U.S, and thus a much larger domestic pool from which to draw potential talent. Though, as Lee Kuan Yew observed, the U.S. effectively supplements its relatively smaller domestic population through immigration, and by doing so enlarges its potential talent pool to the entire world, giving America a competitive advantage over China. There are, however, a few assumptions, and perhaps misconceptions, inherent in Lee Kuan Yew's assessment.

To begin with, Lee Kuan Yew was not advocating that the U.S. grow its population through mass immigration to match the size of China's population, or even suggesting the U.S. would need to do so to counter China. Though there are some advocating for this, it would only serve to exacerbate the significant downsides of immigration that America has already experienced, such as disrupting social cohesion and flooding the labor market to the detriment of the existing populace. Nor is it necessary to receive the maximum competitive advantages and benefits from immigration. It is not sheer numbers of immigration according to Lee Kuan Yew that gave the U.S. the advantage; otherwise, China would have the advantage. Instead, what matters is the ability to attract the most talented immigrants from around the world.

This leads to two significant conclusions. First, U.S. immigration policies should directly target and cater to highly talented immigrants. Second, America must be open to and attractive to talented immigrants from around the world. This is particularly important as other countries are also competing for these same talented immigrants. In short, America must seek to recruit the best and brightest from the world's population to work in and for America, just as a sports team recruits the best players to win games.

China fully understands this, which is why they aggressively pay for talent through their Thousand Talents Program. America must do the same through its immigration policies. In relation to the New Cold War, this means recruiting highly skilled immigrants in STEM-related disciplines. These are the players whom America needs to win. As such, America must adopt immigration policies that prioritize highly skilled immigrants in these areas over other forms of immigration.

To do so, the U.S. immigration system must be recalibrated towards the recruitment of highly skilled immigrants. Other countries already do this, notably, Canada and Australia, which have merit-based immigration systems, and in contrast to America, prioritize immigration based on employment rather than family connections. America must do the same. Existing barriers to recruiting and retaining foreign-born talent must also be eliminated.

America should not only shift towards a more merit-based immigration system generally, but also leverage and reform existing programs like the H-1B visa program for highly skilled workers. Currently H-1B visas for high-skilled workers are capped at 85,000 a year, and employer demand has exceeded supply since 2004.[42] To realize the fullest benefits from immigration, America cannot allow the best players to go elsewhere, especially not as the result of an arbitrary cap. That said, in the past, the program has also been abused by certain employers to circumvent hiring otherwise equally skilled Americans in favor of less expensive foreigners, and as a mechanism to outsource American jobs. As such, the program must be reformed to ensure that American workers are always prioritized while at the same time ensuring foreigners with valuable skills filling legitimate needs in high-tech industries are not turned away. Encouragingly, significant bipartisan steps have recently been made in this direction.[43]

It is equally senseless that great American universities educate highly skilled foreign workers in STEM disciplines, and when they want to stay and work in America, they are forced out. This must change. These highly skilled immigrants in STEM fields must not only be provided the means to stay and work in the U.S. but also be given an expedited pathway to becoming U.S. citizens so that they are fully invested in America's success.

Focusing on highly skilled immigrants will also make immigration generally more popular with the U.S. public, providing an even more welcoming environment for immigrants overall, which will in turn help the U.S. to continue to attract them. Prioritizing highly skilled immigrants mitigates many of the downsides of immigration. For while highly skilled immigrants compete against U.S. citizens as well, they do not depress wages or take jobs from U.S. citizens in the same way, or to the same degree, as immigrants on the lower skilled side. In fact, they are more likely to bring capital to start businesses, create jobs, and invest in America. Highly skilled immigrants are also unlikely to enter the country illegally or to utilize America's welfare system. To the contrary, highly skilled immigrants likely pay higher taxes and provide a net financial benefit to U.S. coffers, thereby decreasing the overall burden on the welfare state. As a result, high skilled immigration has not caused the same societal problems and frictions as other forms of immigration. For example, U.S. citizens rarely complain about having too many foreign-born tech workers or doctors, and according to a 2018 survey by the Pew Research Center, roughly eight in ten U.S. adults support encouraging highly skilled people to immigrate and work in the U.S.[44]

In addition to prioritizing highly skilled immigrants, other forms of immigration must be curtailed to offset the increase in high skilled immigration. Illegal immigration must be curbed completely. This includes severely punishing U.S. employers who knowingly engage in the hiring of illegal immigrants and doing everything necessary to secure America's borders. For as President Ronald

Reagan correctly observed, "a nation that cannot control its borders is not a nation." If this does not occur, Americans will turn against all forms of immigration, as many have already begun to do.

Some U.S. businesses will undoubtedly claim that without vast amounts of low-cost immigrant labor, prices will rise, and consumers will ultimately be harmed by paying more for products. Similar arguments are made by proponents of cheap Chinese exports. Not acknowledged, however, is that U.S. citizens pay for low wage immigration through the additional burdens placed upon the welfare system and public resources. In this regard, while Americans may not always see it, they are paying significantly through higher taxes and stretched public services. These same businesses also argue that low wage immigrants do jobs Americans will not. This is untrue, or more precisely, wrongly stated. What they mean is that low wage immigrants do certain jobs for less money than U.S. citizens are willing to accept to perform those same jobs. If paid more for these jobs, however, many more Americans would willingly perform them. Thus, the issue is one of business not wanting to pay more, not Americans' unwillingness to do those jobs.

Furthermore, when not provided with an alternative and forced to do so, industry will adjust to labor shortages by coming up with creative solutions and investing in the creation of their future workforce. As Oren Cass sets forth in his excellent book *The Once and Future Worker*:

> "A strange facet of the modern immigration debate is the tendency of the same pro-business interests that typically wax lyrical about free-market dynamism to lament in apocalyptic terms the prospect of a limited supply of labor. But the result of such [a] limit is not, generally, economic ruin. Instead, businesses reorient themselves toward using the

labor that is available. Investment goes toward making jobs more attractive and boosting productivity."

To illustrate this point, Mr. Cass cites the example of Home Depot. In 2018, fearing that a shortage of construction workers would slow spending on new homes, Home Depot announced a ten-year partnership with the Home Builders Institute to invest $50 million in training twenty thousand additional workers.

Thus, by taking away the ability to rely on the importation of low-cost immigrant labor, industry will, for lack of any other choice, reorient and invest in the domestic workforce, ultimately to the benefit of America and its workers. For as Sun Tzu said in *The Art of War*:

> "Confront them with annihilation, and they will then survive; plunge them into a deadly situation, and they will then live. When people fall into danger, they are then able to strive for victory."

In short, whether it be an army or a company when forced to find a way to survive, a way will be found.

Another argument as to why the U.S. should reduce low wage immigration is automation. As automation grows, there will simply be less need for low wage immigrant workers in the U.S., as many of the jobs currently performed are increasingly being performed by machines. Moreover, by continuing to rely on the importation of low-cost labor, the U.S. is deterring and delaying necessary investment into labor-saving technology and automation that can bring manufacturing back to the U.S., which will ultimately create higher paying jobs for American citizens.

Finally, America cannot simply rely on immigration for talent, to the exclusion of its home-grown population. Domestic and global talent policies must go together. America cannot be fully dependent on immigration for its talent, such as in STEM fields, while under-investing in cultivating its domestic supply. Like relying on foreign based supply chains, this will put America in a weak and vulnerable strategic position. And while the U.S. should most certainly supplement its population through high skilled immigration, it must prioritize its existing citizenry first and foremost. Otherwise, the U.S. stands to lose the patriotism and national cohesion required to defeat China. It should never be forgotten that a nation is far more than simply an economy or a marketplace.

CHAPTER 7
WARFARE

"In peace prepare for war, in war prepare for peace. The art of war is of vital importance to the state. It is matter of life and death, a road either to safety or to ruin. Hence under no circumstances can it be neglected." – Sun Tzu, *The Art of War*

"A prince ought to dedicate himself to no other art, nor study anything other than war with its rules and discipline. This is the sole art that is expected of rulers." – Niccolo Machiavelli, *The Prince*

An ancient maxim states: "if you want peace, prepare for war." In essence, it means that strong nations with strong militaries are unlikely to be attacked by others, while weak nations with weak militaries are constantly threatened. Or, as put even more bluntly by Thucydides: "the strong do what they can and the weak suffer what they must."

As nuclear armed superpowers able to destroy themselves and the world many times over, it is unlikely that America and China will engage in all out armed conflict, though it certainly cannot be ruled out. Regardless, the balance of military power will matter greatly, as it did during the first Cold War, even without armed conflict between the two nations. If China perceives that it has equaled or surpassed the U.S. in military capabilities, it will grow more assertive in other strategic areas, especially within its own geographic region, where it has hegemonic designs. This will put U.S. strategic assets and allies at risk and weaken U.S. power and influence around the world. It is therefore imperative that America possesses the world's strongest military and can continue to project power around the globe.

Not only must America strengthen traditional military capabilities, but also, it must enhance capabilities in other forms of warfare. Like China, the U.S. must view national defense and warfare from a whole of government standpoint. This is especially important in the age of high-tech warfare, where entirely new battlefields and ways of waging war have emerged. It is also where America is increasingly falling behind China.

High-Tech Warfare

Americans widely believe that they possess the world's greatest military and would defeat China in an armed conflict. They would be shocked to know that this is not necessarily true. To the contrary, in war games conducted by the U.S. military over the last decade, the U.S. consistently loses to China.[45] Shocked Americans will undoubtedly wonder how this could possibly be, especially as the U.S. spends massively on its military. Indeed, the U.S. spends more on national defense than the next ten countries combined, to the tune of well over $700 billion annually.[46] It is not, however, the amount being spent, but the way that is at issue.

While China has relentlessly modernized its military, incorporating state of the art high-tech weaponry and systems, the U.S. military has fallen behind technologically. This is persuasively detailed in the book *The Kill Chain: Defending America in the Future of High-*

Tech Warfare, by Christian Brose, former staff director of the Senate Armed Services Committee and close adviser to the late Senator John McCain. *The Kill Chain* sets forth in alarming detail how the U.S. military's edge has been eroded by Russia and China, and how America—the world's preeminent military power since the end of the first Cold War—grew complacent.

As Brose explains, China continued to upgrade its military and plan for the high-tech wars of the future, while America fought the wars of the past, expending enormous resources on increasingly outdated weapons, systems, and methods of conducting war. America also fought for decades against relatively lesser enemies, like the Taliban, ISIS, and Al Qaeda, who though undoubtedly ruthless and resourceful enemies, were undeveloped in their military capabilities. Already far superior, the U.S. military hardly needed to upgrade technologically to defeat them.

China not only modernized its military utilizing the latest technology, but also developed it with America firmly in mind. Following the advice in *Unrestricted Warfare,* China developed so called Assassin's Mace weapons. In Chinese folklore, Assassin's Mace Weapons allow an inferior power to defeat a seemingly superior adversary by striking at its weaknesses. And as Michael Pillsbury explains in *The Hundred Year Marathon,* China spent billions to "make a generational leap in military capabilities that can trump the conventional forces of Western powers."

America must immediately pivot away from places like the Middle East and prepare for a great power war with China. This will be a different kind of war than those in the Middle East, or those against rogue states and non-state actors. It will require a different kind of military. In the age of high-tech warfare, the U.S. military must also think and act differently than in the past. This requires a different kind of organization, one that can innovate, adapt, and react quickly to rapidly changing technology. The current rigid, risk averse, and overly bureaucratic U.S. military structure is ill-fitting in this regard. This is particularly true when it comes to the U.S. military's agonizingly slow, complex, and byzantine weapons acquisition system.

Military experts, including the late Senator John McCain, blame the U.S. weapons acquisition system for the U.S. military's losing its technological edge to China and Russia. [47] Largely unchanged since the 1960's, this antiquated system accrues to the benefit of vested interests, those ingrained in the so-called military-industrial complex. The system's notoriously onerous requirements, with paperwork alone taking months, if not years, deters new and innovative entrants while preventing disruptive new technologies from moving forward. This is clearly evidenced by most current major defense acquisition programs being legacy weapon systems designed to fight 20th century wars.[48] The acquisition system must be reformed and streamlined to align with the speed, flexibility, and agility required of modern high-tech warfare. In this regard, the U.S. military should learn from and emulate innovative tech companies, which operate in an environment where today's state of the art technology is obsolete tomorrow and moving fast and taking risks is necessary to stay ahead of the curve. This requires quick decision making and action, not months or years of bureaucratic review.

Reform of the weapons acquisition system must be part of a larger comprehensive military modernization program similar in size, purpose, and urgency to the one that President Reagan implemented to defeat the Soviets in the first Cold War. And indeed, realizing the dire need for reform, former President Trump took significant steps in this direction.[49] The reforms, however, must continue, if not accelerate, and must go much further still. The U.S. military must quickly move away from military relics of the past and legacy programs no longer effective in the age of high-tech warfare. They must instead concentrate on integrating future technologies like artificial intelligence, advanced manufacturing, and the Internet of Things into military applications. As Brose argues in *The Kill Chain*, military spending must be focused on creating state of the art high-tech integrated platforms, systems, and battle networks that can coordinate and accelerate the military's ability to identify and understand a target, decide how to attack the target, and carry out the act of destruction of the target. Maximizing the "kill chain" will require incorporating and capitalizing on future technologies.

To accomplish this goal, the U.S. military should work closely with tech companies in Silicon Valley, just as it did with industry during the first Cold War. To that end, the current hostility between the military and Silicon Valley must change for the good of the country. Indeed, it should be a natural partnership, as Silicon Valley was built on a foundation of public-private partnerships between the national security and technology communities.[50] But over the last decade, the partnership has frayed. It is critical for U.S. national security that the relationship be repaired, especially as technological innovation has rapidly shifted from government labs to commercial companies. China understands this and is working closely with its own tech firms; indeed, Chinese tech firms are required by law to work with China's government and military. America's own tech companies must feel a similar obligation to work with the U.S. military.

As part of the modernization process, the U.S. military must focus on building and advancing autonomous weapons. In the modern age, loss of human life is increasingly unacceptable, and the American public quickly sours on any conflict where there are a high number of U.S. casualties. Soldiers are also extremely expensive to outfit and train. The U.S military should therefore rely more heavily on developing high-tech autonomous weapons, including expendable drones and planes not requiring a human pilot. Not only will this protect against an unacceptable loss of human life and save money, but also, it will allow the U.S. military to explore new and innovative combat strategies.

U.S. military spending and personnel should be reprioritized to recognize the changing terrain of warfare. Combat is no longer confined to physical space, or even Earth. Indeed, in many ways, outer space will define the future of warfare, with satellites critical for everything from communications, gathering intelligence to guiding precision bombs, missiles, and drones. War with China may very well be won or lost in space. Already, both China and Russia have weaponized space in ways that put existing U.S. space capabilities at risk, and by extension U.S. military and defense capabilities. [51]The recent creation of a new U.S. military branch, Space Force, acknowledges the importance of outer space for military purposes and is a step in the right direction. Partnerships with innovative American space companies like Space X and Blue Origin are also of great importance and should be deepened.

Cyberwarfare

Another critical domain in the age of high-tech warfare is cyberspace, increasingly a battlefield with real world and national security implications. It could even be said that America and China are already at war in the cyber realm, with China using cyberwarfare daily to attack America.

China has poured enormous resources into cyberwarfare, and as a result, China's cyberattacks are becoming ever more frequent and difficult to stop. As society becomes more digital and connected, the potential devastation of these cyberattacks will only grow, with the potential to knock out critical infrastructure and military installations and create chaos. Furthermore, cyberattacks have the advantage of not arising to acts of war, as traditionally defined, operating in a sort of grey area. There is also a level of deniability, with cyber-attacks difficult to trace or conclusively attribute, making retaliation less justifiable in the eyes of the public or the world, which only adds to their appeal and effectiveness.

In many respects, the U.S. is currently a sitting duck for China's cyberattacks. With near impunity, China is using cyberat-tacks, and cyber hacking, to steal valuable and sensitive data from the U.S. government, companies, and the public. To better defend against these attacks, the U.S. must strengthen the nation's digital infrastructure and security. The U.S. must also go on the offen-sive in the cyber realm, for as they say, the best defense is a good offense. And if ever hoping to deter them, the U.S. must inflict significant costs on China and others for cyberattacks. The U.S. must see cyberattacks for what they are—acts of warfare. And it must respond accordingly.

Despite cyberwarfare's increasing importance and prevalence, the U.S. does not spend nearly enough on it, with the vast majority of defense spending still going to more conventional warfare capabil-ities. And in relation to China, America is being woefully outspent and outmaneuvered in the cyber realm.[52] Instead of buying more planes and bombs, the U.S. military needs to invest in enhancing its cyber capabilities. This means focusing on and adequately resourc-ing Cyber Command. U.S. military training in general must also change to recognize the importance of cyber warfare and integrate it into all operations. In addition, the U.S. military is woefully short on cyber-savvy personnel. To rectify this, the U.S. military must recruit talented tech personnel from America's top technology uni-versities, while pursuing strategic partnerships with America's tech companies, which possess perhaps the best potential cyberwarfare capabilities and personnel in the world. Moreover, the U.S. military should target and cultivate a different sort of military personnel than in the past by recruiting tech savvy youngsters more adept and inclined towards playing video games than storming beaches. To that end, the U.S. military must change its recruitment strategies and messaging to cater to and attract these individuals.

Information Warfare

In conjunction with developing cyber capabilities, the U.S. must increase its overall information warfare capabilities as well. Information warfare should be defined broadly and holistically, to include the interplay and integration of electronic warfare, cyberwarfare, and psychological operations, in short, controlling, affecting, and manipulating communications for strategic purposes.

In the first Cold War, America utilized information warfare to devastating effect to undermine and weaken Soviet power and influence both domestically and around the world. But since the end of the first Cold War, America has not focused on information warfare to the same degree. As a result, its once formidable capabilities have waned. This has caused America to miss strategic opportunities presented by the rise of the internet and social media which have allowed information warfare to become exponentially more effective and widespread. America must understand again how integral information warfare is to national security.

To its credit, under the Trump Administration, there was a renewed focus on the importance of information warfare. But America must go further still. Information warfare campaigns against China must be both overt and covert, targeting all facets of Chinese power, including those countries and potential allies China wishes to influence. The U.S. should use information warfare to erode China's reputation and standing in the world; seek to identify and exploit fault lines in the Chinese public, sowing dissent, confusion, and chaos; and seek to undermine and discredit China's leaders, and their authority, in the eyes of the Chinese public.

Accomplishing these goals, however, requires a deep understanding of Chinese language and culture. It is said that China is very good at interpreting U.S. communications, but that America, lacking in speakers of Mandarin, is flying blind in China's communications. In the first Cold War, America had Sovietologists and studied Kremlinology to understand the inner workings of Soviet politics and interpret Soviet communications and actions. America requires the same for China.

Understanding China and its leaders also requires spy craft and intelligence work. For as Sun Tzu said in the *Art of War*:

> "The reason the enlightened prince and the wise general conquer the enemy whenever they move and their achievements surpass those of ordinary men is foreknowledge."

Sun Tzu understood the great importance of using intelligence, or as he called it foreknowledge, in defeating an adversary. The CCP understands this as well and is voracious in intelligence gathering efforts against America and its allies.

In many ways, China has become far better at intelligence than America. Seeing its tremendous value and usefulness, China applies intelligence gathering in nearly every domain, whether military, social, or commercial. For example, the CCP uses espionage to steal commercial trade secrets and intellectual property from U.S. companies; places and recruits moles in U.S. universities and academia to steal critical research; and through United Front operations, employs the Chinese diaspora throughout the world as operatives to obtain intelligence. China uses any means and anyone it can for its intelligence gathering efforts. According to James Olson, former

CIA chief of counterintelligence and author of the book *To Catch a Spy: The Art of Counterintelligence*, the CCP makes "regular use of diplomatic, commercial, journalistic, and student covers for their operations in the United States," and aggressively uses "Chinese travelers to the U.S., especially business representatives, academics, scientists, students, and tourists, to supplement their intelligence collection."[53]

By contrast, U.S. intelligence services have struggled to counter China in intelligence gathering and spy craft. This is partly due to America being an open society, which China fully exploits to its advantage, while China is a closed society, making intelligence gathering against it far more difficult. U.S. intelligence services have also been caught by surprise at the sheer breadth and scope of Chinese intelligence gathering efforts, especially as they significantly progressed over the last decade.

The U.S. must become far more adept at intelligence work relating to China, both in terms of stopping China's intelligence gathering against the U.S. and enhancing America's ability to gather intelligence from China. This will require a renewed focus on the importance of intelligence gathering in the New Cold War and a different approach involving not simply U.S. intelligence services and government entities but the private sector as well. Like China, the U.S. must take a whole of government approach to intelligence, with far greater coordination between U.S. intelligence services and private companies.

The U.S. should also fully leverage the Five Eyes network against China. Created after World War II, the Five Eyes is an intelligence alliance composed of the United States, the United Kingdom, Canada, Australia, and New Zealand. The Five Eyes was used to great effect during the first Cold War and should be employed again in the New Cold War, including expanding the alliance to add additional member countries that can benefit from and enhance the alliance and its intelligence gathering efforts against China.

War by Other Means: Economic Warfare

To combat China, America must view war in a broader context, looking beyond simply the Armed Forces or traditional military capabilities and notions of warfare, as China does. America must engage in war by other means, combining and utilizing all facets of its hard and soft power across various domains. One of the most important of these is economic warfare.

Economic warfare can be defined as the deployment or utilization of the economy, or economic means, for geopolitical purposes. China has been using economic warfare against the U.S. for decades, and America must respond accordingly. Along with ensuring that America is strong and resilient economically, as discussed earlier, America must also seek to weaken China economically. This is critically important, as the economy is the very foundation of China's power.

Under the Trump administration, America became a more adept practitioner of economic warfare. Former President Trump's preferred mechanism was tariffs, which he placed on hundreds of billions worth of Chinese products as part of a prolonged trade war seeking to rectify China's trade abuses. Tariffs can be an effective tool, useful in rebalancing the trade scales, and Trump's tariffs harmed China economically, perhaps more than the Chinese let on. But there are more effective tools in America's economic warfare arsenal that can and should be wielded against China.

With the dollar as the world's reserve currency, America holds enormous advantages in the domain of economic warfare. China knows this, and has desperately pushed for an alternative reserve currency, including its own, to remove America's advantage. But absent the unforeseeable, the fall of King Dollar is a long way off. And while America possesses the "exorbitant privilege" of the world's reserve currency, it should be leveraged against China.

Through the dollar, America has effective control over the global financial system, granting it vast power not only over domestic entities, but also over foreign entities requiring access to dollar markets. If America wanted, it could deprive China and its banks of access to dollars. This would be incredibly destabilizing for China, as a large percentage of its debt is denominated in dollars. America could also lock China and its banks out of the global financial system through its control over the Society for Worldwide Interbank Financial Telecommunication (SWIFT). SWIFT enables financial institutions to send and receive information about financial transactions, facilitating the international dollar system. In the past, America has used control over SWIFT against enemies like Iran to devastating effect.

Energy provides America with another advantage in economic warfare. America is now an energy powerhouse, while China is both the world's largest energy consumer as well as the world's largest importer of oil and gas. America can exploit this by making energy more expensive and more difficult for China to obtain. In the past, America was forced to keep a close relationship with the Middle East to ensure an adequate supply of oil and natural gas. This meant involvement in messy Middle Eastern politics. Now America is largely energy independent. China must maintain a large supply of energy from the Middle East, which accounts for around 40 percent of China's oil imports, forcing China to take an active role in the region.[54] This gives America opportunities to engage in economic warfare, including disrupting and entangling China in the Middle East, and other difficult places, in strategically detrimental ways.

To further disrupt China economically, America should pull

supply chains out of China. Not only will this secure America and its economy, but also, it will place strain on China's economy and populace, and by extension the CCP, as China has an extremely large population to employ, house, and feed to stave off social unrest. Moreover, this will force China to become more insular, and revert further into its state-controlled economic system, starving out the private sector. This will retard China's economic growth, and breed even greater inefficiencies, causing China to become more like the Soviet Union with the same strategic vulnerabilities.

Further, by ripping supply chains out of China, America can take away some of the CCP's most powerful weapons of political coercion and economic warfare. Currently, the CCP wields enormous power and leverage over both companies and countries by virtue of their control over critical global supply chains. This represents a major vulnerability for not only America but also the entire free world. This must be reversed. And while there will undoubtedly be short term pain and costs as a result, it is a risk worth taking. For though in the short term some goods may become more expensive for Americans and corporations may lose profit, these costs pale in comparison to the long-term costs and consequences of continued American dependency on China. Moreover, the benefits both economically and from a national security perspective of America regaining control over industries and supply chains will be tremendous. Additionally, "decoupling" from China will pose a serious threat to its main source of global influence—the size of its market.

Finally, just as President Reagan effectively kept western technology out of the hands of the Soviet Union during the first Cold War, along with partnering with U.S. tech companies to advance its own military capabilities, America must stop China and its military from obtaining critical technology from U.S. tech companies. This is particularly important as China is still largely reliant on U.S. tech companies for critical technology and components. To that end, the U.S. government should continue to fully utilize and empower the Committee on Foreign Investment in the United States (CFIUS) to block Chinese investment in strategic U.S. technology companies and sectors. America should also block exports of strategic U.S. technology to China through blacklists and sanctions to prevent U.S. companies from selling components or technologies to Chinese companies. Under the Trump administration, the U.S. began to block China's access to semiconductors, a vital technological component. To expand this effort further, not only should the U.S. block additional critical technologies and components from being sold to Chinese companies, but also, it should work with NATO allies like the U.K., Australia, and the E.U. to block predatory Chinese investment in strategic companies and industries in their countries. Creating common and united fronts with allies in this respect will stop China from obtaining strategically important technology with military applications, and hinder China's ability to move up the value chain and challenge America technologically.

CHAPTER 8
FOREIGN POLICY: THE GREAT GAME

"If an enemy has alliances, the problem is grave and the enemy's position strong; if he has no alliances, the problem is minor and the enemy's position weak." – Sun Tzu, *The Art of War*

"War is a highly overrated tool of foreign policy."
– George F. Kennan

Foreign policy brings together many of the areas discussed in this book, which is why it is discussed last. Foreign policy can be viewed as the totality of a nation's strength, including economic, military, political, and soft power, and the wielding and projecting of that strength on the world stage.

The world is changing. The post-Cold War order is crumbling, and a new world order is emerging to take its place. America must adjust to this fact. But while some argue that America should retreat from the world, this would be a strategic mistake. America can and should lead the world. Indeed, it must, or else China will fill the void and mold the world in its image, as it has already begun to do.

China is asserting its strength in the foreign policy arena like never before. It is even adopting an aggressive "wolf warrior" form of diplomacy, based upon a popular Chinese action movie, to bully countries and bend them to its will. China has also systematically infiltrated and taken leadership positions in important multilateral and international organizations to turn them in its own favor, while simultaneously seeking to create rival organizations to build a new Chinese-led world order.

America cannot and should not cede the field to China. For whether America retreats from the world or not, the great game will continue. It is far better for America to stay in and influence the outcome. Moreover, America still has a great deal to offer in its leadership, and much of the world prefers its brand to China's illiberal authoritarianism. But to secure its leadership, America must change how its foreign policy operates. It must engage smartly and strategically with the rest of the world to counter China and its ambitions.

America must craft and effectively implement a foreign policy strategy to combat China. To do this, America needs to think and act long term. China's authoritarian one-party system allows it advantages in this respect. China can develop a strategy and stick with it over decades, while America's democratic, highly partisan two-party system oscillates back and forth and is geared towards more short-term thinking, often dictated by ever-shifting public opinion. But America has shown the capability in the past for long-term grand strategy in foreign policy. During the first Cold War, America successfully developed and carried out the containment strategy against the Soviet Union over several decades. In the new Cold War, America should again pursue long term strategic alliances to contain China. It should also engage in the strategic disruption of China's plans. Or as Sun Tzu puts it in the *Art of War*:

"When the enemy is relaxed, make them toil. When full, starve them. When settled, make them move."

China has gone largely unchallenged for decades, and been allowed to rise and gain strength unimpeded, as it followed Deng Xiaoping's prescient advice to "hide your light, and bide your time." But China also knows it is in a precarious position. It must create new markets for its exports to continue to employ its massive population and subsidize its move up the value chain before it falls into the middle-income trap. It must grow rich before it grows old. It must grow its way out of the enormous debts it has incurred before the house of cards falls. It must secure the natural resources to fuel its economy to keep growing. And perhaps most importantly, it must make the world safe for its authoritarian form of leadership. Before this all occurs, China is vulnerable, which presents America with strategic opportunities to disrupt China's plans and exploit its vulnerabilities.

To seize upon these strategic opportunities, however, America must begin by addressing and strengthening its own foreign policy personnel and apparatus. America has neglected its foreign policy corps, while China has enhanced its own. China has developed highly professional, highly competent diplomats to advance its foreign policy goals. By contrast, U.S. ambassadors to important countries are frequently appointed because they are large campaign donors, not because of their foreign policy expertise. This is strategically stupid and demonstrates a lack of seriousness and commitment to foreign policy and diplomacy. America must develop an army of professional diplomats to rival any in the world. To that end, the U.S. State Department must be well resourced and placed on an equal footing with the Defense Department. For in the New Cold War, they are equally important, and must work in concert to achieve U.S. geopolitical goals.

The Indo-Pacific

In the New Cold War, America must change where and how it deploys its foreign policy resources. While America focused on the Middle East, China focused on gaining and asserting power and influence in its neighborhood in the Indo-Pacific, home to the fastest growing and most consequential markets in the world, and a neighborhood dominated for decades by America.

Understanding its importance, China is leveraging military modernization, influence operations and predatory economics to reorder the Indo-Pacific region to its advantage.[55] China's goal is to achieve Indo-Pacific regional hegemony and displace America from the region. Realizing this, President Obama implemented the much-heralded Pivot to Asia to prioritize the region. However, the pivot was constantly interrupted by Syria, Iran, and other pressing short-term political issues. It was not until recently, under President Trump, that America truly began to refocus on the region.

America still possesses a great deal of goodwill in the region, with many Indo-Pacific nations prospering under the U.S. security umbrella. Many of these nations are also weary of China's rise, especially Japan and Vietnam, which are historical adversaries of China. These countries have seen glimpses of what Chinese regional domination means in China's recent aggression in the South China Sea and crushing of dissidents in Hong Kong. But these countries also understand the reality of China residing in their backyard, while America is an ocean away. China understands this, too. This forces Indo-Pacific nations to continually weigh and measure the relative strengths and weaknesses of the two superpowers in the region and position themselves accordingly. As a result, past allegiances and partnerships are becoming weaker as nations hedge their bets. This makes it critically important for America to maintain a significant presence in the region to counter China's growing influence and aggression. The Trump Administration's free and open Indo-Pacific Strategy presented a solid start in this regard.

America must not simply seek to counter China militarily in the region, however, but also economically. Acknowledging this fact, the Trump Administration emphasized the economic components of its Indo-Pacific policy through initiatives such as the Better Utilization of Investment Leading to Development, or BUILD Act, and creating a new U.S. development agency, the U.S. International Development Finance Corporation (USIDFC), to leverage private sector investment in low-and middle-income countries in the Indo-Pacific. The Asia EDGE initiative was a U.S. effort to grow sustainable energy markets throughout the region.

While the BUILD Act and Asia EDGE represent a good start, China is still putting far more economic resources into the region by comparison. China's Belt and Road Initiative (BRI) is a trillion-dollar project, while the BUILD ACT, touted as the U.S. response to BRI, is only a drop in the ocean by comparison. This must change. America must be a major driver of economic development in the region to counter and compete with China. To do so, America must not only prioritize the region economically but also reallocate resources currently being employed in places like the Middle East and others of lesser strategic importance and deploy them to the Indo-Pacific. America should also join with allies and other stakeholders in the region such as Japan and Australia to coordinate, drive, and amplify economic development opportunities in the region to compete with those offered by China.

Indo-Pacific nations will be watching U.S. commitment to the region closely. Any perceived erosion of U.S. credibility in supporting allies or inability to provide a viable alternative to the economic opportunities offered by China will force nations to reconsider their relationship with the U.S. and move closer to China. America must therefore continually demonstrate commitment to the region. A good step in this regard would be for America to re-enter the Trans-Pacific Partnership (TPP). By renouncing TPP, America forfeited a leadership role in establishing multilateral rules and institutions for regulating trade in the region, and which also accounts for one-third of all world trade.[56] This is something that China—understanding the strategic bullet it dodged—called a grand gift. It also laid significant doubts concerning U.S. commitment. Returning to the TPP will lay some of those doubts to rest.

Soft Power

China has formed alliances with U.S. adversaries including Russia, Venezuela, and Iran, as it pursues the ancient adage that the enemy of my enemy is my friend. Along with being U.S. enemies, these nations are led by authoritarian governments. A key theme of the New Cold War will be Democracy vs. Authoritarianism. Countries with authoritarian governments will naturally align with China, as communist nations once aligned with the Soviet Union. This trend is already playing out as China seeks to export its authoritarian governance model to the world.

While alliances with other authoritarian governments may serve China's strategic hard power interests, they can also serve to diminish China's soft power. The term soft power was coined by Joseph Nye to mean the ability to shape another state's policies and actions through attraction and persuasion. This can include the allure of a nation's cultural appeal to the world. For example, U.S. soft power during the first Cold War persuaded other nations to join it, as popular American music and movies swept across the world. Ideals such as the American Dream and the Shining City on the Hill attracted people to America. Increasingly, soft power plays a critical role in foreign policy. China understands this and has tried desperately to increase its soft power with decidedly mixed results. America should do everything it can to maximize its own soft power, while diminishing China's.

As it did with the Soviet Union in the first Cold War, America should cast the New Cold War in clear terms of Good vs. Evil and Freedom vs. Oppression. America should label China, as President Reagan did the Soviet Union, as an Evil Empire. To further this narrative, Hollywood should be enlisted and weaponized to brand the CCP as bad actors in the eyes of the American public and the world at large. Hollywood did this to great effect with the Soviet Union, and before that with Imperial Japan and Nazi Germany. Additionally, America should continue to fully expose China's abhorrent human rights violations, including against the Uighurs, an ethnic Muslim minority in China, millions of whom the CCP has interned in re-education camps, put into forced labor, and sterilized. America must continue to bring these atrocities to light. Doing so will hopefully end them, while also causing countries and companies around the world to turn away from China.

Xi Jinping has fostered and stoked nationalism in China to solidify his power. Chinese films like Wolf Warrior 2, depicting Chinese heroes defeating American bad guys, have become huge hits in China, capitalizing on this growing nationalism, and even inspiring China's diplomats to engage in "wolf warrior" diplomacy. But it is a dangerous game. And Chinese nationalism has been compared to a tiger that the CCP has fed and now is forced to ride, for fear that if they get off the tiger, it will eat them. This provides America with opportunities to diminish China's appeal around the world.

Sun Tzu advised, "if your opponent is of choleric temper, seek to irritate him." And indeed, America should do just that, especially as China has shown itself to be very thin skinned. To that end, America can and should force actions undermining the great power narrative that the CCP has created and the Chinese people have come to believe. This will put the CCP in domestic political peril as the Chinese populace punishes its leaders for any perceived weakness. By forcing the CCP to bend to the will of its nationalist populace and become ever more aggressive as a result, America can also maneuver China into detrimental positions not in China's long-term strategic interests. This will harm China's goal of increasing its soft power and influence throughout the world, making it a place that other countries are increasingly uncomfortable with, as any legitimate dispute with or criticism of China is met with antagonism meant to satisfy a nationalistic domestic audience. This is a phenomenon that countries like Australia, Japan, and Canada have already come to experience firsthand. And indeed, China's aggressive nationalism, mishandling of the COVID-19 pandemic, and "wolf warrior" diplomacy have already begun to have a negative effect on how the world views China, with unfavorable views of China recently reaching historic highs in many advanced countries.[57] America should capitalize on this fact.

Alliances

Winston Churchill famously said, "There is only one thing worse than fighting with allies, and that is fighting without them." Undoubtedly, as Churchill recognized, there are risks and rewards that come from alliances. America has understood this since its earliest days as a nation. Indeed, the Founding Fathers warned repeatedly of "entangling alliances" pulling the country into unnecessary conflicts. But all in all, America's alliances have served it well. And America's unprecedented network of alliances and partnerships since World War II represents a strategic advantage against China.

The CCP has learned the lessons of the Soviet Union's demise and is keenly aware of how America and its huge alliance system successfully executed the containment strategy against the Soviet Union. To avoid a similar fate, China is doing all that it can to divide and conquer U.S. allies and ensure that it is not seen as a common enemy like the Soviet Union was during the first Cold War.

To counter China, America must continue to strengthen traditional western alliances with, among others, the E.U., Australia, Canada, and the U.K. To their credit, all have recently pushed back against China's advances as they have grown concerned with its intentions. This is evidenced in their rejection of predatory state-backed Chinese investment in strategically important companies and industries and recent blocking of Huawei from their 5G infrastructure. The E.U. has even gone so far as to designate China a "systemic rival."[58] The more closely these countries align with America and provide a united front against China, the better.

It is therefore imperative that the U.S. blunt and counter the economic opportunities and financial enticements presented to these countries, and their companies, by China and its massive market. As discussed earlier in this book, China has fully weaponized its economy, and any and every economic tie with China is used as leverage by the CCP to control and influence other countries. The CCP is systematically attempting to deepen economic ties, whether through trade, investment or otherwise, with U.S. allies for this purpose. And in many ways, they are succeeding. China is now the largest trade partner for many U.S. allies, including the E.U., which even recently entered into a comprehensive investment agreement with China.[59]

As such, America must not only continue to strengthen alliances like NATO, but must also enter into mutually beneficial trade and investment agreements with allied nations and create economic blocs with common multilateral institutions and market standards. This will shift economic power away from China and back to the U.S.

and its partners, which will join together to create a market dwarfing the size of China's. Not only will this disrupt China's economic advances, but also, it will either freeze China out of a large portion of the global economy or force China to play by rules advantageous to America and its allies. Either way, it inures to America's benefit.

Moreover, for U.S. alliances to be sustainable and effective they must also be mutually beneficial and to the extent possible reciprocal. Allies therefore cannot simply free ride on the U.S. military for their defense, as in the past. This is no longer acceptable, or indeed with the rise of China and its military capabilities, sufficient. America can and should be the leader in alliances such as NATO, but allies must also have significant skin in the game and live up to their commitments. For instance, NATO allies should be spending 2 percent of their gross domestic product on defense, as previously agreed. This will not only make NATO stronger, but also will ultimately bind it more closely together.

However, to be a nation that other nations want to follow and ally with, America must also be consistent and trustworthy. If other nations view America as changeable and fickle, they will not ally with America for fear that agreements made today will be undone tomorrow. As a one-party authoritarian state without political opposition, China possesses certain advantages in this respect. However, China has also shown a propensity for not following through on its promises. And while America has shown itself to be a reliable ally through the years, that perception is changing as America becomes more politically polarized domestically. As a result, other countries, even longtime allies, are becoming unsure of America's commitment. America must correct this perception, or China will exploit it, as indeed it has already begun to do.

Unlike America, China is bordered by either unfriendly nations, or in the case of North Korea, highly unstable ones. To the degree possible, America should seek to stir up chaos and turmoil around China's borders. This will serve to keep China preoccupied in its own backyard, causing it to expend resources closer to home, rather than utilizing them to project power around the world, or against America. To that end, it is critically important for America to build and maintain alliances with the other traditional powers in China's backyard, including India, Australia, South Korea, and Japan. Of these countries, India is perhaps the most important. Indeed, a strong alliance between India and America is China's nightmare.

India shares a land border with China and has long been thought of as a potential counterweight to China. India rivals China in size and population and has a historically contentious relationship with China. This was highlighted in June 2020 by a bloody border dispute in the Himalayas where Chinese and Indian troops clashed, and dozens died.[60] America should exploit the growing animosity between India and China by fully supporting India and deepening economic and military ties. America should also continue to strengthen and enhance the quadrilateral security coalition (The "Quad") with the U.S., Japan, Australia, and India, creating a potential Indo-Pacific NATO right at China's doorstep.

Speaking of China's doorstep, no issue animates the CCP's ire more than Taiwan. Though Taiwan is ostensibly an independent nation with its own democratically elected government, the CCP views the island as a runaway Chinese province. Even the mere mention of Taiwan as a separate country infuriates the CCP. President Xi has made returning Taiwan to China a central focus of his "China Dream" and "Great Rejuvenation." The biggest obstacle standing in the way of Xi's goal is America and its longstanding support for Taiwanese independence.

Taiwan represents not only a critical U.S. ally in China's backyard, but one whose very existence directly challenges Xi's great power narrative. This gives Taiwan tremendous strategic and symbolic value. Nothing undermines the CCP more than Taiwan as a thriving independent democracy, open market economy, and strong U.S. ally. That is the very antithesis of the CCP. Taiwan also serves as a barometer for the U.S.'s overall strength and influence in the region relative to China, and one closely watched by other nations in the region. The U.S. must therefore do all it can to ensure that Taiwan continues to thrive as an independent nation.

To that end, along with continuing to provide Taiwan's army with training and selling Taiwan advanced defense systems and weaponry to significantly drive up the costs to China of an attempted forcible retaking of Taiwan, the U.S should unequivocally reiterate its commitment to defending Taiwan by entering into a mutual defense treaty. Additionally, the U.S. should further solidify economic and diplomatic ties with Taiwan by entering into a mutually beneficial trade agreement. The more formal links exist between the U.S. and Taiwan, the more difficult it will be for China to forcibly retake it. In addition, such ties will enhance U.S. credibility, strength, and influence in the region.

Finally, as America strengthens its own alliances, it must also seek to disrupt and weaken China's alliances. This is particularly true of America's longtime adversary from the first Cold War, Russia. For as Sun Tzu said in *The Art of War*:

> "Thus, what is of supreme importance in war is to attack the enemy's strategy. Next best is to disrupt his alliances; do not allow your enemies to get together."

A strategic alliance between China and Russia against America poses a serious threat. Alone, each is a formidable challenger to U.S. power. Together, they are nearly overpowering from a military standpoint.

To a significant degree, however, the marriage between Russia and China is one of convenience predicated on America as a common enemy. But it is an uneasy friendship, given the long history between the two countries. And though greatly reduced from its heyday as a Soviet empire, Russia is a proud country that still views itself as a great power. How long will it accept junior status to China in an alliance, especially as China encroaches further into Russia's territory and perceived sphere of influence, and forces Russia to enter one-sided energy deals?

America should seek to create a wedge between the two countries by implementing information warfare campaigns aimed at the Russian populace to stir up nationalist sentiments related to Russia's perceived subservience to China. Russia is not accustomed to playing junior partner, especially not to China, which was once a Russian client state. America should prey on Russia's insecurities, highlighting its junior-partner status and its geographic vulnerabilities to stoke Russian fear and resentment of China among the Russian populace. Ironically, it was America's ability to drive a wedge between China and the Soviet Union that played a significant role in the Soviet Union's downfall in the first Cold War. America should help Russia return the favor in the New Cold War.

Ultimately, a nation's foreign policy, like much else, begins at home. Domestic strength begets strength abroad. And even the greatest foreign policy strategies in the world will fail without complimentary domestic policies to buttress them, or a public willing to support them.

U.S. leaders must therefore continually emphasize the importance of foreign policy to the American people as it relates to China, with the link between foreign policy and domestic consequences well established. Like the Soviet Union in the first Cold War, the U.S. public must fully understand the necessity of foreign policy in countering China in the New Cold War. And this understanding must be solidified in the minds of Americans, so it withstands changes in leadership and transcends partisan politics.

Strong and successful countries will also not follow or ally with countries that are not themselves strong and successful. America's ability to implement and carry through with the domestic polices discussed throughout this book will matter greatly for its strength internationally, and by extension, for its ability to counter China in the foreign policy arena. This is especially true if China continues growing economically, while America stagnates or declines economically. For just as people naturally look toward the rising sun and not the setting one, so do other countries. America must therefore show in all ways that its star is still ascendant. Domestic strength through innovation, economic dynamism, and widespread prosperity will ensure that this continues to be the case.

CONCLUSION

"Shall we expect some transatlantic military giant to step the ocean and crush us at a blow? Never! All the armies of Europe, Asia, and Africa combined, with all the treasure of the earth (our own excepted) in their military chest, with a Bonaparte for a commander, could not by force take a drink from the Ohio or make a track on the Blue Ridge in a trial of a thousand years. At what point then is the approach of danger to be expected? I answer. If it ever reach us it must spring up amongst us; it cannot come from abroad. If destruction be our lot we must ourselves be its author and finisher. As a nation of freemen we must live through all time or die by suicide." – President Abraham Lincoln, Lyceum Address

"Great civilizations are not murdered. They commit suicide."
– Arnold Toynbee

As set forth in this short book, China has embarked on a long-term whole of government strategy to weaken and overtake America, a strategy carried out successfully while America has been distracted. The CCP has concentrated its plans on defeating America because they know that it is the only nation capable of stopping China's rise to global domination. America can no longer look the other way or appease China for the sake of economic gains. To do so would be an historic mistake, and one the CCP is betting on.

China is rushing forward to seize the strategic window of opportunity to become the world's dominant nation, hoping America will not stop it before China has grown too powerful. Nazi Germany made similar calculations during WWII, as Hitler sought to keep America from entering the war while the Nazis accumulated power and territory and defeated their enemies. Nazi Germany nearly succeeded in this regard, until America was at long last awoken from its slumber, and with its allies, succeeded in saving the world from Nazism. Now America must fully rouse to the China threat and do what needs to be done to win. For the threat is just as grave, and the hour equally late.

To that end, America must be wary of China's attempts to stall for time by offering potential carrots, such as potential cooperation on combating climate change, in exchange for America relenting from acting against it. China knows that if it is unchallenged over time it will continue to grow stronger, while America grows weaker. As such, China will attempt to persuade America to stop, while continuing itself to advance. This is a well-practiced technique of the CCP. America must guard against it and be unwavering in combating China.

Just as China has taken a whole of government approach against America, America must in turn take a whole of government, if not whole of nation approach to combating China. This requires America to think and act strategically, whether in its economy, education, immigration, military, or foreign policy. America must become inwardly and outwardly strong and resilient, both to protect itself from China's attacks and to counter China effectively on the world stage. This means that significant changes must be made. Not all will be easy, or without cost. But they must be done, and sacrifices must be made. To do otherwise will mean a world where China is ascendant and America is in decline—a world darker, crueler, and far less free. The stakes could not be higher.

To accomplish what needs to be done, America must be unified. It must be strong and resilient as a society. A divided America cannot defeat China. When there are riots in U.S. cities, it weakens American power, prestige, and influence around the world, while providing China plenty to exploit. When America cannot enforce its own laws and control its own borders, it looks weak and feckless. And when America's political system appears in disarray, it turns countries away from the American system and towards China's authoritarian system. Internal divisions, whether political, racial, economic, or otherwise, weaken America more than any outside threat. America is its own worst enemy, a fact not unnoticed by China or others seeking America harm.

Over the years, America has grown ever more polarized and divided as a nation, rife with ideological and partisan differences. Americans have always engaged in vigorous, often rancorous debate concerning the important issues of the day. But there was an underlying fundamental agreement about the country that kept it all together. Now even that is being lost, as the traditional American values that provided the bedrock for America's greatness are questioned by many, or worse, denigrated and discarded. A growing number of Americans even see America as a fundamentally evil country built upon a tainted and tarnished legacy, a country rotten right from its very founding to the point where Americans are wrong for simply being American, and patriotism is equated to bigotry. This is not healthy for a country or a society, and certainly not conducive to defeating an opponent like China.

Every country has that which in its past is shameful. America is no exception. Slavery is a deep stain that can never be washed away. But just as one must acknowledge the bad with the good, one must also acknowledge the good with the bad. On balance, America has been a great force for good in the world. Without America, Nazi Germany and the Soviet Union would have triumphed, and the world would be a far worse place. And to so many in so many different places, America has stood, and continues to stand, as a beacon of freedom and hope, a bright light in an otherwise dark world. There is much to be proud of America for, and good reason why it has long been considered the leader of the free world.

That said, criticisms would not find their appeal if there were not issues that needed to be addressed in America. Certainly, there are. Americans do not possess the same sense of community in many places that they once did. The social institutions that bound people together into a community, such as churches or civic organizations, are not as relevant. People feel increasingly disconnected from one another, and from their own country. This is exacerbated by the many manufacturing towns decimated due to outsourcing to China and other low-cost labor countries. These places and their people have been left behind by globalization, abandoned along with their jobs. This caused a ripple effect as it broke up families and feelings of dignity and pride were replaced with the numbness of opioids. Towns and cities like this exist throughout America. Once great symbols of U.S. manufacturing might, they are reduced to sad forgotten shells.

It is unacceptable that so many places have been abandoned the way they have, betrayed by their own country and its leaders, who allowed their jobs to be outsourced, or taken by low-cost labor, and received nothing in return. It is no wonder these places fell into despair and addiction. As part of the industrial policy discussed in this book, these places must be prioritized. America should incentivize companies and businesses to invest in these areas, to bring back what China and others have taken from them. These towns and cities should become once again manufacturing strongholds and emblems of American power. This will not only be right but will also have deep symbolic value. It will represent an America returning to its people. An America that puts its citizens first.

To achieve unity and social cohesion, America must embrace what unites rather than what divides. It must share the common goal of national pride for the country that all Americans call home. For that to happen, there must be a sense of unified purpose and collective destiny once again. Without this the big hard things that need to be done to combat China will be impossible, and the country will be driven further apart, balkanized, as certain politicians stir divisions for political gain. Perhaps the China threat can be the catalyst for that unified purpose. There is hope in this regard, with an emerging consensus in America on the threat of China. It is perhaps the one area of agreement in America's highly partisan politics. To implement an effective long-term national security policy against China, this must continue over and into successive administrations.

I have no illusions that this short book, or the analysis herein, nearly equates to or will have anywhere close to the effect of George Kennan's famous Long-Telegram, which brought wide attention to the true extent of the threat posed by the Soviet Union and communism in the first Cold War and set forth the containment strategy to defeat them. I do hope, though, that on some level this book brings greater attention to the direness and enormity of the China threat to America, and that perhaps, in some small way, it illuminates the actions necessary for America to overcome it. At least, that is my great hope and reason for writing this book.

I believe unapologetically in America and its greatness. I believe it is unique in its history. It is a special place of providence that can rise to any challenge and defeat any enemy. And while the road will be undeniably long and hard, and China is a competitor unlike any faced previously, it is a challenge America can meet and must overcome.

READING LIST

The Art of War by Sun Tzu

Wealth of Nations by Adam Smith

The Prince by Niccolo Machiavelli

The Republic by Plato

Destined for War: Can America and China Escape Thucydides' Trap? by Graham Allison

Lee Kuan Yew, The Grand Master's Insights on China, the United States, and the World by Graham Allison.

From Third World to First: The Singapore Story -1965-2000 by Lee Kuan Yew

On China by Henry Kissinger

The World Turned Upside Down: America, China, and the Struggle for Global Leadership by Clyde Prestowitz

China, Trade and Power: Why the West's Economic Engagement with China Has Failed by Stewart Paterson

The Hundred-Year Marathon: China's Secret Strategy to Replace America as the Global Superpower by Michael Pillsbury

Stealth War: How China Took Over While America's Elite Slept by General Robert Spalding

The Return of Great Power Rivalry: Democracy versus Autocracy from the Ancient World to the U.S. and China by Mathew Kroenig

CEO, China: The Rise of Xi Jinping by Kerry Brown

Innovation Economics. The Race for Global Advantage by Robert D. Atkinson and Stephen J. Ezell

The Kill Chain: Defending America in the Future of High-Tech Warfare by Christian Brose

Unrestricted Warfare: China's Master Plan to Destroy America by Qiao Liang and Wang Xiangsui

The China Dream: Great Power Thinking and Strategic Power Posture in the Post-American Era by Liu Mingfu

Has China Won?: The Chinese Challenge to American Primacy by Kishore Mahbubani

Red Flags: Why Xi's China Is in Jeopardy by George Magnus

The Party: The Secret World of China's Communist Rulers by Richard McGregor

Deng Xiaoping and the Transformation of China by Ezra F. Vogel

On War by Carl von Clausewitz

War by Other Means: Geoeconomics and Statecraft by Ambassador Robert D. Blackwill and Jennifer M. Harris

Xi Jinping: The Backlash by Richard McGregor

The Globotics Upheaval: Globalization, Robotics, and the Future of Work by Richard Baldwin

AI Superpowers: China, Silicon Valley, and the New World Order by Kai-Fu Lee

The Once and Future Worker: A Vision for the Renewal of Work in America by Oren Cass

To Catch a Spy: The Art of Counterintelligence by James Olson

Freedom's Forge: How American Business Produced Victory in World War II by Arthur Herman

Clashing over Commerce: A History of US Trade Policy (Markets and Governments in Economic History) by Douglas A. Irwin

ACKNOWLEDGEMENTS

I must begin by thanking my beautiful, talented, and amazing wife, Allison, who inspires me every day to do great things and be a better person, and who is gracious enough to put up with me.

Next, I would like to thank my mom who has always encouraged me to write. When I was a boy, she bought me a set of Encyclopedia Britannica including the Great Books of Western Civilization which began my love of reading and history.

I would also like to thank my brother, Mark, who along with being a terrific brother and friend is the smartest person I know. His achievements never cease to amaze and make me want to constantly improve myself.

Finally, I would like to thank all the teachers I have had throughout the years. I was not always the best student, and certainly in many cases not the best behaved, of which I am sorry, but I learned something from all of you, and for that I am eternally grateful.

NOTES

1 Tang, Frank. "China overtakes US as No 1 in buying power, but still clings to developing status." *South China Morning Post*, South China Morning Post Publishers Ltd., 21 May 2020, https://www.scmp.com/economy/china-economy/article/3085501/china-overtakes-us-no-1-buying-power-still-clings-developing

2 Cimmino, Jeffrey, and Matthew Kroenig. "The China Challenge." *Atlantic Council,* 16 December 2020, https://www.atlanticcouncil.org/content-series/atlantic-council-strategy-paper-series/the-china-challenge/

3 Salam, Reihan. "Normalizing Trade Relations With China Was a Mistake." *The Atlantic*, Atlantic Media Company, 8 June 2018, https://www.theatlantic.com/ideas/archive/2018/06/normalizing-trade-relations-with-china-was-a-mistake/562403/

4 Bosco, Joseph. "The Historic Opening to China: What Hath Nixon Wrought?" *Harvard Law School Harvard National Security Journal Online Edition*, 25 September 2015, https://harvardnsj.org/2015/09/the-historic-opening-to-china-what-hath-nixon-wrought/

5 "Text of Clinton's Speech on China Trade Bill", Federal News Service, March 9, 2000.

6 Autor, D, D Dorn and G H Hanson (2016), "The China Shock: Learning from Labor Market Adjustment to Large Changes in Trade." *Annual Reviews of Economics*, 8: 2015-240.

7 Mason Jeff, and Lawder David. "Trump targets China in call for WTO to reform 'developing' country status." *Reuters*, 26 July 2019, https://www.reuters.com/article/us-usa-trade-wto/trump-targets-china-in-call-for-wto-to-reform-developing-country-status-idUSKCN1UL2G6

8 Guilford, Gwynn. "Hank Paulson on the Chinese economy, Xi Jinping, and what Americans don't get about China." *Quartz*, Quartz Media, Inc., 15 April 2015, https://qz.com/383295/hank-paulson-on-the-chinese-economy-xi-jinping-and-what-americans-dont-get-about-china/

9 Sempa, Francis. "Forget About a 'New' Cold War. The Old One Never Ended. James Burnham and 'The War We Are In' with China." *The Diplomat,* Diplomat Media Inc., 27 May 2020, https://thediplomat.com/2020/05/forget-about-a-new-cold-war-the-old-one-never-ended/

10 Cordesman, Anthony. "From Competition to Confrontation with China: The Major Shift in U.S. Policy." *CSIS, Center for Strategic & International Studies,* 3 August 2020 https://www.csis.org/analysis/competition-confrontation-china-major-shift-us-policy

11 Wray, Christopher. "The Threat Posed by the Chinese Government and the Chinese Communist Party to the Economic and National Security of the United States." 7 July 2020. https://www.fbi.gov/news/speeches/the-threat-posed-by-the-chinese-government-and-the-chinese-communist-party-to-the-economic-and-national-security-of-the-united-states

12 O'Brien, Robert. "The Chinese Communist Party's Ideology and Global Ambitions." 26 June 2020. https://www.whitehouse.gov/briefings-statements/chinese-communist-partys-ideology-global-ambitions/

13 Barr, William. "Transcript of Attorney General Barr's Remarks on China Policy at the Gerald R. Ford Presidential Museum." 17 July 2020, https://www.justice.gov/opa/speech/transcript-attorney-general-barr-s-remarks-china-policy-gerald-r-ford-presidential-museum

14 Pompeo, Michael. "Communist China and the Free World's Future." 23, July 2020, https://www.state.gov/communist-china-and-the-free-worlds-future/

15 Gan, Nectar. "Xi Jinping Thought – the Communist Party's tighter grip on China in 16 characters." *South China Morning Post,* South China Morning Post Publishers Ltd., 25 October 2017, https://www.scmp.com/news/china/policies-politics/article/2116836/xi-jinping-thought-communist-partys-tighter-grip-china

16 Blanchette, Jude. "From "China Inc." to "CCP Inc.": A New Paradigm for Chinese State Capitalism." *China Leadership Monitor*, 1 December 2020, https://www.prcleader.org/blanchette

17 Blanchette, Jude. "From "China Inc." to "CCP Inc.": A New Paradigm for Chinese State Capitalism." *China Leadership Monitor*, 1 December 2020, https://www.prcleader.org/blanchette

18 Hernandez, Javier, Guo, Owen, and Mcmorrow, Ryan. "South Korean Stores Feel China's Wrath as U.S. Missile System Is Deployed." *The New York Times*, The New York Times Company, 9 March 2017, https://www. nytimes.com/2017/03/09/world/asia/china-lotte-thaad-south-korea.html

19 "Daryl Morey backtracks after Hong Kong tweet causes Chinese backlash." *BBC News*, 7 October 2019 https://www.bbc.com/news/business-49956385

20 "China's Attacks on Australian Goods Take Many Different Forms." *Yahoo! Finance*, Bloomberg News, 17 December 2020, https://finance. yahoo.com/news/china-attacks-australian-goods-many-210001348.html

21 "'Made in China 2025' to Focus on Ten Key Sectors," *People's Daily Online*, May 22, 2015, http://en.people.cn/n/2015/0522/c98649-8895998.html

22Girard, Bonnie. "Chinese Government-Paid Scientists Plead Guilty to Stealing Research From an American Children's Hospital." *The Diplomat*, Diplomat Media Inc.,8 August 2020 https://thediplomat.com/2020/08/ chinese-government-paid-scientists-plead-guilty-to-stealing-research-from-an-american-childrens-hospital/

23Girard, Bonnie. "Chinese Government-Paid Scientists Plead Guilty to Stealing Research From an American Children's Hospital." *The Diplomat*, Diplomat Media Inc.,8 August 2020 https://thediplomat.com/2020/08/ chinese-government-paid-scientists-plead-guilty-to-stealing-research-from-an-american-childrens-hospital/

24 Rogin, Josh. "NSA Chief: Cybercrime constitutes the "greatest transfer of wealth in history" *FP Foreign Policy*, The Slate Group, 9 July 2012, https:// foreignpolicy.com/2012/07/09/nsa-chief-cybercrime-constitutes-the-greatest-transfer-of-wealth-in-history/

25 "How China's Economic Aggression Threatens the Technologies and Intellectual Property of the United States and the World." White House Office of Trade and Manufacturing Policy, June 2018 https://www.white-house.gov/wp-content/uploads/2018/06/FINAL-China-Technology-Report-6.18.18-PDF.pdf

26 "Threats to the U.S. Research Enterprise: China's Talent Recruitment Plans." Staff Report, Permanent Subcommittee on Investigations, United States Senate, https://www.hsgac.senate.gov/imo/media/doc/2019-11-18%20PSI%20Staff%20Report%20-%20China's%20Talent%20Recruitment%20Plans.pdf

27 Mozur, Paul. "Beijing Wants A.I. to Be Made in China by 2030." *The New York Times*, The New York Times Company, 20 July 2017, https://www.nytimes.com/2017/07/20/business/china-artificial-intelligence.html

28 Mozur, Paul. "Beijing Wants A.I. to Be Made in China by 2030." *The New York Times*, The New York Times Company, 20 July 2017, https://www.nytimes.com/2017/07/20/business/china-artificial-intelligence.html

29 Woo, Stu. "In the Race to Dominate 5G, China Sprints Ahead." *The Wall Street Journal,* Dow Jones & Company, Inc., 7 September 2019 https://www.wsj.com/articles/in-the-race-to-dominate-5g-china-has-an-edge-11567828888

30 Delaney, Robert. "Kissinger urges greater cooperation with China as 'the world's centre of gravity' shifts." *South China Morning Post*, South China Morning Post Publishers Ltd., 27 September 2017, https://www.scmp.com/news/china/policies-politics/article/2112957/kissinger-urges-us-boost-cooperation-beijing-massive

31 Abi-Habib, Maria. "How China Got Sri Lanka to Cough Up a Port." *The New York Times*, The New York Times Company, 25 June 2018, https://www.nytimes.com/2018/06/25/world/asia/china-sri-lanka-port.html

32 Rogin, Josh. "China's efforts to undermine democracy are expanding worldwide." *The Washington Post*, 27 June 2019, https://www.washingtonpost.com/opinions/2019/06/27/chinas-efforts-undermine-democracy-are-expanding-worldwide/

33 Ma, Josephine. "Chinese Communist Party wraps up top policy meeting by outlining plans for nation to become greater power." *South China Morning Post,* South China Morning Post Publishers Ltd., 29 October 2020, https://www.scmp.com/news/china/politics/article/3107660/chinese-communist-party-wraps-top-policy-meeting-outlining

34 Sandlund, William. "China's Retrograde Rural Land Policies." *Council on Foreign Relations*, 5 August 2020, https://www.cfr.org/blog/chinas-retrograde-rural-land-policies

35 Guilford, Gwynn. "Hank Paulson on the Chinese economy, Xi Jinping, and what Americans don't get about China." *Quartz*, Quartz Media, Inc., 15 April 2015, https://qz.com/383295/hank-paulson-on-the-chinese-economy-xi-jinping-and-what-americans-dont-get-about-china/

36 Brenan, Megan. "Congress' Approval Drops to 18%, Trump's Steady at 41." *Gallup*, Gallup, Inc., 30 July 2020, https://news.gallup.com/poll/316448/congress-approval-drops-trump-steady.aspx

37 Bentley, Zak. "UK to Launch Infrastructure Bank in Spring 2021." *Infrastructure Investor*, PEI Media, 26 November 2020. https://www.infrastructureinvestor.com/uk-to-launch-infrastructure-bank-in-spring-2021/

38 Herman, Arthur. "America's STEM Crisis Threatens Our National Security." *American Affairs*, American Affairs Foundation Inc., Spring 2019 / Volume III, Number 1 https://americanaffairsjournal.org/2019/02/americas-stem-crisis-threatens-our-national-security/

39 M. Martel, J. Baer, N. Andrejko and L. Mason, Open Doors 2019 Report on International Educational Exchange (New York, NY.: Institute of International Education, 2019), pp. 8; 39-40; 62.

40 Zwetsloot, Remco, and Peterson, Dahlia. "The US-China Tech Wars: China's Immigration Disadvantage." *The Diplomat,* Diplomat Media Inc., 31 December 2019, https://thediplomat.com/2019/12/the-us-china-tech-wars-chinas-immigration-disadvantage/

41 Zwetsloot, Remco, and Peterson, Dahlia. "The US-China Tech Wars: China's Immigration Disadvantage." *The Diplomat*, Diplomat Media

Inc., 31 December 2019, https://thediplomat.com/2019/12/the-us-china-tech-wars-chinas-immigration-disadvantage/

42 Editorial Board. "Trump's Immigration Choice." *The Wall Street Journal,* Dow Jones & Company, Inc., 16 June 2020 https://www.wsj.com/articles/trumps-immigration-choice-11592350847

43 "Bipartisan Group of Lawmakers Propose Reforms to Skilled Non-Immigrant Visa Programs to Protect American Workers." The office of Senator Chuck Grassley, 22 May 2020. https://www.grassley.senate.gov/news/news-releases/bipartisan-group-lawmakers-propose-reforms-skilled-non-immigrant-visa-programs

44 Connor Phillip, and Ruiz Neil. "Majority of U.S. Public Supports High-Skilled Immigration." *Pew Research Center,* 20 January, 2019, https://www.pewresearch.org/global/2019/01/22/majority-of-u-s-public-supports-high-skilled-immigration/

45Pickrell, Ryan. "The US has been getting 'its ass handed to it' in war games simulating fights against Russia and China." *Business Insider*, 18 March 2019, https://www.businessinsider.com/the-us-apparently-gets-its-ass-handed-to-it-in-war-games-2019-3

46 U.S. Defense Spending Compared to Other Countries." *Peter G. Peterson Foundation*, 13 May 2020, https://www.pgpf.org/chart-archive/0053_defense-comparison

47 Levine, Peter. "If You Want More Defense Innovation, Spend Less on Legacy Platforms." *War on the Rocks,* 20 August 2018, https://warontherocks.com/2018/08/if-you-want-more-defense-innovation-spend-less-on-legacy-platforms/

48 Levine, Peter. "If You Want More Defense Innovation, Spend Less on Legacy Platforms." *War on the Rocks,* 20 August 2018https://warontherocks.com/2018/08/if-you-want-more-defense-innovation-spend-less-on-legacy-platforms/

49 Thompson, Loren. "Top Five Steps Trump Has Taken To Prepare The U.S. Military For Whatever Comes Next." *Forbes,* 6 January 2020https://

www.forbes.com/sites/lorenthompson/2020/01/06/top-five-steps-trump-has-taken-to-prepare-the-us-military-for-whatever-comes-next/?sh=38a321662ee5

50 Suciu, Peter. "AFVentures Connects the Military With Silicon Valley." *ClearanceJobs.com,* 12 June 2020. https://news.clearancejobs.com/2020/06/12/afventures-connects-the-military-with-silicon-valley/

51 Zivitski, Liane. "China wants to dominate space, and the US must take countermeasures." *DefenseNews,* Sightline Media Group, 23 June 2020, https://www.defensenews.com/opinion/commentary/2020/06/23/china-wants-to-dominate-space-and-the-us-must-take-countermeasures/

52 Wagner, Daniel. "China's head start in cyberwarfare leaves the US and others playing catch-up." *South China Morning Post,* South China Morning Post Publishers Ltd., 7 March 2019, https://www.scmp.com/comment/insight-opinion/united-states/article/2188873/chinas-head-start-cyberwarfare-leaves-us-and

53 Giglio, Mike. "China's Spies Are on the Offensive." *The Atlantic*, Atlantic Media Company, 26 August 2019, https://www.theatlantic.com/politics/archive/2019/08/inside-us-china-espionage-war/595747/

54 Reuters Staff. "Factbox: Asia region is most dependent on Middle East crude oil, LNG supplies." *Reuters*, 8 January 2020, https://www.reuters.com/article/asia-mideast-oil-factbox/factbox-asia-region-is-most-dependent-on-middle-east-crude-oil-lng-supplies-idINKBN1Z71VW

55 Garamone, Jim. "White House Report Recommends Multi-Pronged Approach to Counter China." *US Department of Defense*, 5 June 2020, https://www.defense.gov/Explore/News/Article/Article/2210283/white-house-report-recommends-multi-pronged-approach-to-counter-china/

56 "Trans-Pacific Partnership: Summary of U.S. Objectives." *Office of the United States Trade Representative,* https://ustr.gov/tpp/Summary-of-US-objectives#:~:text=With%20the%20participation%20of%20Japan,third%20of%20all%20world%20trade.

57 Silver, Laura, Devlin, Kat, and Huang, Christine. "Unfavorable Views of China Reach Historic Highs in Many Countries." *Pew Research Center*, 6 October 2020, https://www.pewresearch.org/global/2020/10/06/unfavorable-views-of-china-reach-historic-highs-in-many-countries/

58 Von der Burchard, Hans. "EU slams China as 'systemic rival' as trade tension rises." *Politico*, 12 March 2019, https://www.politico.eu/article/eu-slams-china-as-systemic-rival-as-trade-tension-rises/

59 Fallon, Theresa. "The Strategic Implications of the China-EU Investment Deal." *The Diplomat*, Diplomat Media Inc., 4 January 2021,   https://the-diplomat.com/2021/01/the-strategic-implications-of-the-china-eu-invest-ment-deal/

60 Gettleman, Jeffrey, Kumar, Hari and Yasir, Samir. "Worst Clash in Decades on Disputed India-China Border Kills 20 Indian Troops." *The New York Times*, The New York Times Company, 16 June 2020, https://www.nytimes.com/2020/06/16/world/asia/indian-china-border-clash.html

About the Author

Lee Steinhauer is an attorney and the President and Founder of The Steinhauer Group, a government and legal affairs firm located in central Florida. Lee lives in central Florida with his wife Allison and his son Alexander.